Buying a Home

DON'T LET THEM MAKE A MONKEY OUT OF YOU!

Alysse Musgrave

8th Edition

Buying a Home/ Alysse Musgrave —8th ed.
ISBN 978-1-7347437-8-4

Contents

To Paul, John, George, Ringo, Bruce, Tina, Jimmy, and Ray.

Also, to Lia, Greg, Bodhi, and caffeine.

Home is the place where, when you have to go there, they have to take you in.

—Robert Frost

Introduction

Let's face it: in a real estate transaction, the buyer assumes most of the risk. The seller walks away from the property, free of obligation and responsibility. The buyer pays for inspections, appraisals, and closing costs, and ultimately ends up with the house—and a big mortgage. At best, buying a home is a complicated process. At worst, it can be an emotional and financial nightmare. It's not just about finding a good house in the right location; you also need to verify its condition, negotiate a fair price, arrange financing and insurance, and take possession, all while ensuring you are buying a home that you will be able to resell for a profit in the future. The logistics and associated stress of homebuying can strain even the toughest individuals.

Before 1989, all real estate agents worked for the seller. An agent would spend days with potential buyers who had no idea that the person showing them homes and buying them lunch had a fiduciary duty (legal obligation) to disclose *everything* they knew about the buyer to the seller. For example, if the buyers casually mentioned they would be willing to pay $50,000 above their current offer for a particular property, the showing agent was legally required to disclose this information to the seller. Would this information affect the seller's negotiation of the transaction? Of course! Would these buyers have been more discreet had they known the person they thought was "their" agent was negotiating against them? Absolutely!

Caveat Emptor (buyer beware) was - and still is - quite literally the law of the land. After years of improper dealings and abuse, disgruntled buyers nationwide realized they were not being treated fairly and filed their grievances in court. As a result of these lawsuits, most states finally implemented mandatory disclosure requirements for real estate agents. That is, agents had to inform buyers and sellers (in writing and in advance) which party the broker would represent: buyer, seller, or both. A band-aid on a bullet wound, at best.

While mandatory disclosures were a step in the right direction, they were not enough to create a level playing field for buyers. Not even close. "Dual Agency" was introduced around this time and was a significant win for traditional real estate brokerages, since it allowed brokers to collect a commission on both the buy and sell sides of the transaction. But it left buyers at a considerable disadvantage. Exclusive Buyer's Agency was born as a result.

Exclusive Buyer's Agents (EBAs) are a subset of buyer friendly real estate agents who vow never to represent sellers or act as dual agents. This group of agents formed a nonprofit organization called the National Association of Exclusive Buyer Agents (NAEBA) to educate, inform, and protect homebuyers' rights. Exclusive Buyer Agency and NAEBA have been a "thing" ever since. Here's the problem: although buyers *can* hire their own Exclusive Buyer's Agent, in most cases, they either can't find one or are unaware that EBAs even exist. Even worse, traditional agents have hijacked the term "Exclusive Buyer's Agent," creating mass confusion for homebuyers, who are left to navigate the process with substandard representation. The complexity of real estate transactions makes homebuyers particularly vulnerable to fraudulent practices by sellers, agents, lenders, and other "professionals." They can only hope that the people involved in their transaction are trustworthy and competent, since they have no way of knowing the difference.

The U.S. consumer real estate market is confusing, broken, and illogical, and there's no easy fix. The TRID-RESPA laws, designed to improve the mortgage and real estate industries, have created as many problems as they have solved. The same can be said of the National Association of Realtors (NAR) settlement resolving antitrust claims brought against them and others in the Sitzer/Burnett class action lawsuit. Fix one, break two—one step forward, two steps back.

In an ideal world, each party to a real estate transaction would pay for its own representation. Dual agency brokerages would be a thing of the past. Commissions would be fixed, since it takes the same amount of work to help someone buy a $600,000 house as to help someone buy a $100,000 house. But enormous overhauls like these aren't easy. Buyers need cash for their down payment and closing costs, so asking them to pay their agent's fee out of pocket is unreasonable. Real estate brokerages won't cut profits or voluntarily change their tried-and-true business models. Flat-fee models don't always work because agents don't know whether a buyer will look at a few houses or dozens. So here the issues lie. Buyers must learn to navigate a homebuying process plagued by rampant deception and fraud, often without proper representation.

It has been said that a good nonfiction book conveys only the necessary information to the reader, and no more. That's what I aim to do in this book. I tell you only what you *really* need to know and omit all unnecessary fluff. You'll notice that I didn't include links to the HUD or Fannie Mae websites. There isn't a glossary with the definitions of a thousand words you don't care about. It's not a book designed to show off how much I know about real estate, or to overwhelm you with information that's not useful to most buyers.

Instead, my goal is to provide essential information that enables homebuyers to make informed choices and recognize—and avoid—fraud or unfair practices. In short, I aim to help readers become victors, not victims, in residential real estate purchases.

So, who am I? My name is Alysse Musgrave, and I am an Exclusive Buyer's Broker, a Mortgage Loan Officer, and the owner of the oldest and most successful Exclusive Buyer's Brokerage in Texas. Since 1995, I have been working diligently to educate homebuyers and protect their rights. In addition to providing exclusive buyer representation and mortgage services, I speak out against regulatory abuse of purchasers and predatory lending practices. Over the years, I have saved my clients many thousands of dollars by ensuring they are treated fairly and equitably. My firm is one of the few real estate brokerages in the United States that share the common goal of creating a level playing field for homebuyers.

This 8th edition of this book has been the hardest to write – by far. Previous editions discussed changes in the industry resulting from the TRID/Know Before You Owe rules (discussed in detail later). This edition describes how those changes are working (or not working) in the field and the net effects on homebuyers and borrowers. Implementing these changes was challenging, time-consuming, and confusing for real estate agents, loan officers, title agents, and consumers alike. So confusing, in fact, that I became a licensed loan officer specifically to learn the mortgage business from the ground up. Changes in residential real estate resulting from NAR's settlement of the Sitzer-Burnett class action lawsuit also forced me to delay this release, as it takes time to incorporate new procedures and judge their efficacy. The net effects of the settlement will be discussed as well.

As in previous editions, I strive in this book to teach you things that no other real estate agent will disclose. You'll learn how to recognize a good floor plan, how to negotiate with the seller, how to get a firm quote from your loan officer, and much more. I hope this guidance provides you with the tools you need for a less stressful homebuying experience—and that your new home brings you years of comfort, happiness, and financial security. If you have questions about the process, you are welcome to reach out to me at Main@HelpUBuyAmerica.com for guidance. Let's get started.

Visit https://bah8.net to download easy to read and annotated documents for many of the items discussed in this book.

CHAPTER ONE

Real Estate Agents

A real estate agent is a person who is licensed to list and sell real estate; a REALTOR® is a member of the National Association of Realtors. A REALTOR® is always a real estate agent, but not every real estate agent is a REALTOR®. In this book, I use the terms "REALTOR®," "Realtor," "real estate agent," and "agent" interchangeably. A real estate "broker" is a Realtor who owns or runs their own brokerage/company. An "agent" is recruited by and works for the broker.

People have come to assume that Realtors have no value, particularly since the Multiple Listing Service (MLS) database of homes for sale is accessible to anyone with an internet connection. It doesn't help that, in general, real estate agents rank just below car salespeople in likeability and trustworthiness. However, the truth is that a good agent can save you tens of thousands of dollars and substantially reduce the risks involved in purchasing a home. A bad one can do the opposite, and *you'll probably be none the wiser.*

Searching online for a home is something you can do on your own. To get inside a house, however, you need an agent. But any monkey can open the door to a house! An agent's value lies in their knowledge of construction, floor plans, pricing, marketability, financing, hazard insurance, title insurance, and surveys, as well as their ability to protect your rights and negotiate a good deal. They can warn you that a house may not appraise or pass inspection. They can interpret surveys and decipher title reports and are not afraid to tell you (gently or not so gently) if you're making a bad decision.

Most agents will agree that it took 7-10 transactions before they felt comfortable with the homebuying process.

> *To think you can buy a home without an agent simply because you read "Homebuying for Dummies", or this book is a big mistake.*

Self-education does not replace professional representation! You need a skilled buyer's agent or a lawyer; in some states, you need both. Buying a home means dealing with sellers, listing agents, inspectors, insurance agents, lenders, title companies, engineers, and others. After contract execution, you'll spend several thousand dollars on a house you don't yet own, and it helps to have someone on your side to help you navigate shark-infested waters.

Types of Agents

When hiring an agent, you need a highly trained, brutally honest, skilled, and experienced career agent. Your cousin's mother-in-law, who sells one or two homes a year, is likely not qualified to advise or protect you. You want a well-respected, experienced agent. Next, you need the right type of representation. You should be familiar with the following types of agents: Exclusive Buyer's Agents (EBAs), Sometimes Buyer's Agents (SBAs), dual agents, seller's agents, single agents, real estate consultants, and discounters. In the following sections, I describe the roles of these agents.

Exclusive Buyer's Agents

An Exclusive Buyer's Agent (EBA) works in an office that never takes listings and does not represent sellers. Since they represent buyers 100% of the time, there is no potential conflict of interest that could jeopardize your negotiating position. To understand the importance of hiring an Exclusive Buyer's Agent, you should first understand "fiduciary duty."

A fiduciary duty is a legal obligation to act solely in another party's best interests. It's the same duty that an attorney owes to their client. When you work with an EBA, they have a legal, fiduciary duty to negotiate on your behalf. Their goal is to help you buy the home of your choice at the lowest possible price and with the best terms. By law, they will owe you the following:

- Loyalty
- Complete confidentiality
- Obedience
- Full disclosure
- Complete accounting for all funds
- Fairness and honesty

Only a single agent (vs. a dual agent) can be a fiduciary. It's simply impossible to have a fiduciary duty to both a buyer and a seller at the same time and in the same transaction.

> *If the agent you hire to represent you works in a traditional real estate office that acts as a fiduciary to the seller, they are not and cannot be an Exclusive Buyer's Agent.*

All the financial good guys, like Ralph Nadar, Dave Ramsey, Suze Orman, and Jane Chatzky, have advocated for Exclusive Buyer's Agencies (EBAs). Hiring one is the single most important thing you can do to protect yourself when buying a home.

Here's the bad news. Less than ½ of 1% of real estate agents across the country work as Exclusive Buyer's Agents and finding one in some areas can be difficult – if not impossible. Why? First, EBAs earn half of what a dual agent earns in any given transaction, making it challenging to convince a real estate agent to work exclusively with buyers. Since we don't take listings, we don't have yard signs, online listing portals, or open houses to generate buyer leads. It's far easier to take a listing, put a sign in the yard, and wait for an uneducated buyer to come along than to attract buyers without the marketing benefits that listings bring. More troubling is that Exclusive Buyer's Agents are held to a higher standard than other Realtors, which requires more training and handholding of their agents. Most EBA offices lack the time and resources to properly train new agents, resulting in recruiting efforts that have been either lackluster or nonexistent. If you're able to find an EBA to represent you, consider yourself very lucky. If not, awareness, education, and knowing when to keep your mouth shut are key.

Sometimes Buyer's Agents

"Sometimes Buyer's Agents" (SBA) is a term I coined to help buyers differentiate between Exclusive Buyer's Agents and dual agents who falsely market themselves as "buyer's agents." SBAs work for traditional real estate brokerages representing buyers and sellers (Re/Max, Keller Williams, Ebby Halliday, Redfin, Century 21, etc.), often in the same transaction. You can spot a Sometimes Buyer's Agent when they ask you to agree – in writing – to "designated agency," "dual agency," or to the use of "intermediaries," or "transactional agents," discussed later.

A Sometimes Buyer's Agent represents buyers – sometimes. They also represent sellers – sometimes. And sometimes they represent both the buyer and the seller in the same transaction (a dual agent). They flip, and they flop, changing their story depending on who's on the other end of the phone and which house they are showing you. *This is the way the vast majority of agents work.*

So, what's wrong with being an SBA? Nothing, if you're the agent or their broker who stands to benefit financially from a higher sales price. But when you're the buyer – watch out. Your SBA buddy, who is negotiating *for* you this week, may negotiate *against* you the next, and you could end up paying a lot more for your home.

> *Sometimes Buyer's Agents are neither your fiduciary nor your friend, regardless of how often they send you cookies or calendars; they owe you nothing. Read that again!*

Here's another problem. Sometimes Buyer's Agents often have financial incentives and pressure to sell in-house listings. A RE/MAX agent can sell a

Keller Williams listing, for example, but they might receive a $1,500 bonus if they sell a home listed with their own brokerage. They get phony accolades like 100% Club or Million Dollar Producer if they sell enough in-house listings, giving them even more incentive to sell you a particular home. You can bet that these "achievements" will be posted in every ad, social media profile, webpage, and portal where they market their "success." Traditional dual agent offices also favor the seller far more than the buyer, as evidenced by ads touting how much they have "sold." They aim to sell the most real estate at the highest possible price. High volume matters. High sales prices matter.

If you want a high pressure, stereotypically sleazy salesperson to help you buy a home, this is the way to go. But I suspect that's not what you want. As a buyer, you don't want to be "sold" or pay a higher price. You want to buy – for less – and without getting ripped off!

Dual Agents/Intermediaries

A dual agent is one who works for the buyer and the seller in the same transaction. It's comparable to a single lawyer representing both the husband and the wife in a divorce. Crazy, right?

> *A real estate broker cannot simultaneously negotiate the highest price for the seller and the lowest price for the buyer. It's impossible.*

Dual agency is illegal in nearly every other industry, yet it continues to persist in real estate. In my view, and in the eyes of most consumer advocates, it's a form of fraud. Unbelievably, dual agency is perfectly *legal* in ALL states EXCEPT the following: Alaska, Colorado, Florida, Kansas, Maryland, Oklahoma, Texas, and Vermont. But does that mean that it doesn't exist in these states? Hardly. Should a Texas Realtor, for example, wish to sell a seller/client's house to one of their buyer/clients, they use a third party *in their own office* to handle negotiations for one of the parties. This party is called an *intermediary*. The intermediary's job is to negotiate the price and terms of the real estate transaction *without advising either party.* The broker, of course, still earns a double commission on a single transaction.

Process that information for a moment. From the seller's perspective, they are paying a real estate broker *thousands* of dollars to sell their home, but their agent can't help them negotiate a higher sales price. Buyers are on their own with respect to pricing, property condition, and negotiations. They sign a lengthy, restrictive buyer's representation agreement, only to be turned over to an intermediary. The intermediary can provide the buyer with a list of homes that have sold in the neighborhood, for example, but they can't suggest a fair sales price or draft a contract that favors them. They can provide them with a list of home inspectors, but they won't advise them to walk away from a property due to its condition or recommend which repairs to negotiate. The parties are on their own. The agents become order takers, and the buyer and seller foot the bill. It's no wonder consumers hate Realtors.

The following scenario illustrates what it's like to work with a Sometimes Buyer's Agent, dual agent, or intermediary (technically, all the same thing). Suppose you drive by a house that interests you and notice a We're the Best Realty! sign in the yard. You call the number on the sign, and a very nice real estate agent answers.

> *The homeowners hired this Realtor to sell their property and negotiate the highest possible price on their behalf.*

The listing agent offers to show you the house, so you schedule a time to meet and view the listing. They explain that buyers are now *required* to sign a buyer's representation agreement before they can show you a home. The agent reassures you that the agreement will only be binding for the houses they show you, so you sign on the dotted line, since you *really* want to see the house. After the tour, you like the house but are not quite ready to move forward. The agent offers to show you other homes you might like, and they are added to the agreement.

> *Initially, the agent represented the seller. When they show you their seller/client's home, they will represent both you and the seller if you sign a buyer's rep agreement. When they show you another agent's listings, they would act either as a Sometimes Buyer's Agent or as a dual agent/intermediary if the listing is held by someone in their office. If they show you a home listed by another brokerage, they would be acting as your agent. Clear as mud, right?*

In the meantime, they've asked you tons of questions and have a clear picture of your purchasing power and motivation. If you decide to buy the first house they showed you or any of their other listings, they must turn you over to someone else *in their office* (the intermediary/dual agent). However, they would still be legally obligated to tell their seller/client everything they know about you. And, from the seller's perspective, the agent used their house to generate buyer leads. The seller most likely shared all their secrets with this agent, only to have that information used against them if both the buyer and seller sides of the transaction are handled in-house with the same broker. It's a convoluted mess, and it is unfair to both the seller and the buyer; the only people who win here are the dual agent Realtor and their broker.

Real Estate Consultant/Fee for Services

Real estate consultants typically offer à la carte services to buyers. For example, instead of paying a commission based on the home's sale price, a seller can pay a consultant a fixed fee to list the home on the MLS or provide a market analysis. Buyers can pay an agent a fee to write the purchase contract or to show them a specific home. This can be (in very specific circumstances) a great way for real estate to be bought and sold, and more real estate agents are beginning to offer these à la carte services.

Be aware that most agents who work this way require payment in advance for these services, and rightfully so!

Single Agents

A single agent is a broker or agent who represents buyers only, or sellers only, OR both buyers and sellers, but not in the same transaction. When representing the buyer, the agent can't show homes listed by their own brokerage unless the buyer forfeits their right to a proper buyer/client fiduciary relationship. The same is true on the seller's side. The seller's home can't be shown to a buyer whom their firm represents. An outside broker must bring the buyer to the transaction, or the parties must agree to forfeit their fiduciary relationships. Single agency - in my opinion - should be the norm in real estate. I'm hopeful that we get there.

Discounters & Rebaters

Most Realtors detest the idea of discounting their commission; I don't. If buyers perform some of the legwork, they are entitled to a share of the commission. I am comfortable working for less if I can do less work, since that allows me to represent more buyers or to take some time off when I need it.

Many discounters are rebating commissions because they can't compete with other agents in their area; they can only compete on price. Some discounters are online-only brokers whom you never meet and who never see the house you are buying; they only prepare the contracts. Or they might be a local brokerage that hires low level, unskilled (but licensed) hourly workers to show homes and offers buyers cash back at closing. They don't represent you and are not obligated to negotiate on your behalf. They aim to sell the house for the highest possible price since a higher price means a larger commission.

My advice is to steer clear of these types of agents. Far, far away.

If you can find a busy career agent who will reduce their commission by offering a reduced level of service – but still act as your fiduciary and offer you advice and guidance – it can be a great way to buy a house. A good agent, however, will not do the same amount of work for less money. And, as a buyer, it's always a bad idea to put your financial future in the hands of the lowest bidder.

How to Find a Great Agent

With so many licensed Realtors in most markets, you'd think finding a good agent would be a snap. It's not. The market is flooded with wannabe agents who find the real estate lifestyle appealing. There are underpaid teachers with summers off, burnt out corporate employees, career women turned stay at home moms seeking respite, kids fresh out of college, and many others who never even contemplated a career in real estate until their Big Broker agent next door recruited them into the business. While the number of licensed real estate agents is enormous, the number of full-time, dedicated career agents is relatively small.

The biggest problem – particularly for buyers – is that an appalling number of these agents are untrained, undertrained, or untrainable. Since nearly all brokerages focus their training on sellers and how to obtain listings, many Sometimes Buyer's Agents are not taught to do much more than open a door. Very little time is spent on learning what matters to the buyer. So, how do you find a skilled buyer's agent to represent you effectively? Here are some tips.

How to Find an Exclusive Buyer's Agent

Finding an EBA can be tough, so consider yourself lucky if you do. The National Association of Exclusive Buyer's Agents (https://NAEBA.org) can send you a free list of EBAs and/or buyer-friendly agents in your area. Consumer Advocates in American Real Estate (https://CAARE.org) can do the same. You can contact my office at main@HelpUBuyAmerica.com, and we'll try to find someone for you. You can also try https://BuyersAgentSearch.com, but be forewarned. They have an aggressive follow-up system and will drive you crazy with calls, texts, and emails. I don't know about you, but I've never been a fan of the aggressive follow-up. Lastly, search for "exclusive buyer's agents" in your area using your favorite search engine.

Personal Referrals

Most happy buyers and sellers like to reward their agent by referring their friends and family. My business is 90% referral-based, and I take great care to ensure that buyers who are referred to me are treated exceptionally well. (Is there anything worse than referring someone to your friends, only to have egg on your face when they don't perform as expected?)

But friendships and personalities aside, many people – buyers in particular – don't really know how well their agent performed because it's hard to quantify. Was the advice they received solid? Did they overpay because the agent doesn't know how to price property accurately, or isn't a good negotiator? Your best friend may have purchased a beautiful house, but don't assume the agent is good. Research them online and meet with them in person, just as you would with any other agent. Don't feel obligated to use a particular agent just because of your friendship. Just ask for the referral without letting them make introductions. You can take it from there.

Referral Services

Dozens of websites will "match" you with a good agent. Realtor.com, Zillow, Homes.com, MyAgentFinder.com, and Upnest.com are just a few of the agent/consumer matching services. These sites make money (a *lot* of money!) by selling advertising to real estate agents. A well-known financial advisor charges real estate agents, loan officers, insurance agents, and other providers of financial and home services *hundreds* of dollars per month, PLUS 30% or more of the commission earned on the sale, just for sending a few names to a buyer who happens to fill out a form on their site. Zillow Premier Agents can spend $15K or more PER MONTH to be at the top of the list of agents in their market. Every time you look at a house on a site that shows listings, you become a "hot lead." Your email and search criteria are captured, and your information is sold repeatedly to hungry or naïve real estate agents, loan officers, and insurance providers. Are the agents truly vetted, and are they any better than agents not listed on this site? Absolutely not! However, it's a good starting point when you haven't found an agent you like.

If you do find an agent through one of these sites, consider this. The gross commission on a $400,000 sale, assuming a 3% commission to the buyer's agent, is $12,000. At closing, a 30% referral fee, or $3,600, goes to the referral service, leaving the agent with $8,400. Most agents work under a broker, who may take 20-30% of their net commission to hold their license. Very quickly, a $12,000 commission becomes $6,720 (at 20%), *before taxes and expenses,* and about $5,000 in take-home pay. That's not bad when a buyer purchases a house quickly, but it can take many months for buyers to find and close on a home. I have had buyers in my pipeline for over a year!

When an agent's hourly rate drops from workable to negligible, working with you becomes less appealing. Will your agent abandon you midway through your search? Probably not, assuming they are professional and like working with you. But until payday, agents work as volunteers. Like you, we have bills to pay and kids to put through school, and we need to spend our time with buyers who will ultimately let us accomplish our personal financial goals. When you're respectful of your agent's time and appreciative of their efforts, they will work like a mule to help you buy a home. When you're not, it's adios to you and on to the next buyer. My point? If you're lucky enough to find a great agent, treat them well. They don't earn as much as most people think.

Online Search

Conducting an online search is undoubtedly a great way to research and create a short list of agents to interview, but don't rely solely on the *number* of reviews or transactions; they don't tell the whole story. Many new-construction sales, for example, don't appear on the MLS and are not reflected in an agent's sales history. Some sites, like Zillow, allow agents to bundle their reviews, so when you see an agent with hundreds of 5-star reviews, many of them are reviews for a team member or even an admin. Agents leave reviews for other agents they have worked with to help promote their businesses, and agents with the biggest pockets pay to have their name at the top. Most website plugins allow customers to filter out negative reviews, displaying only 5-star ratings that weren't earned.

Take the time to read what people are saying about your agent, and don't just look at the number. It's easy to spot the real ones from the fakes; play it safe by throwing out the highs and lows to get a balanced view of the agent's skills.

Interviewing Agents

Take the time to meet a prospective agent in person before deciding to work with them; a phone interview is a good start, but it's never enough. Pay attention to how they interact with you before, during, and after your meeting. Did they respond to you promptly (within a few hours) when you reached out? Did they ask questions about what you're looking for and where? Did they ask about your pre-approval status? Did they confirm your appointment and show up on time? Are they giving you a canned sales presentation written by their broker, or do they really know what they are talking about? Did they ask you relevant questions? Do they have experience in the area you wish to buy? A good agent will vet you just as you vet them. They should verify your identity and meet you in person before bringing you into someone's home or putting themselves in a potentially unsafe situation.

Equally important: Do you like them? What does your gut tell you about this agent? The agent/buyer relationship can be a long one, and your personalities need to "click" to some degree. Imagine spending weeks or months looking at homes with someone you don't like (or who doesn't like you). It's unpleasant! Here are some questions you can ask prospective agents:

How Long Have You Been in Business?

Ideally, you need an agent with 3-5 years' experience *working with buyers*. I emphasize this because some agents who have been licensed for 20 years have never helped anyone buy a home.

Will you be showing me homes?

Don't be surprised if you call an experienced, seemingly highly productive real estate "team" who sends you a newly licensed Sometimes Buyer's Agent to show you homes. Many agents, especially listing agents, dislike working with buyers, so the job often goes to the new agent who needs to pay their dues. The truly experienced team members will probably never see the house you want to buy. *That's not okay!*

A newer agent who works closely with a highly skilled broker is acceptable, provided their primary duty is to open the door and provide preliminary information. After you've found a house you like, the experienced agent should visit the property with you, help you negotiate a deal, and write an offer.

Whom do you represent?

Most agents will say that they represent both buyers and sellers, sometimes simultaneously. Some will say that even though they work in a traditional real estate office, they only work with buyers or are their team's buyer specialist.

Regardless of what they say, if they are not an Exclusive Buyer's Agent or Single Agent, they can represent both sides. It is imperative that I make this point clear.

Most (but not all!) states require that an agent disclose who they represent at your first "substantive" meeting, usually in writing. This is your opportunity to discuss this important issue in greater detail.

How do you handle competing buyers?

What happens if the agent has a buyer looking for the same type of house as one of their other buyers? Who gets the first look at the property, and what happens if both buyers want to make an offer? My policy is not to represent two clients seeking the same type of property, as I don't want them to compete with one another. Just as an agent can't represent both the buyer and seller in the same transaction, a buyer's agent can't simultaneously negotiate the lowest price on behalf of two separate clients.

How do you handle in-house listings?

There are incentives for KW agents, for example, to show KW-listed homes. How will they handle this conflict of interest when you want to buy a home listed by someone in their office? How do they handle representing both the buyer and seller in the same transaction? Will you be turned over to another agent to handle your negotiations? What happens to the private information that you've shared, which could affect your negotiating position? It's vital that you understand their procedures and don't let anyone convince you it's not a big deal. It is. It is a very big deal.

How will you notify me of new listings?

Most offices offer auto-search, which automatically sends new listings to clients as soon as they are entered into the MLS. Buyers can view photos online, take virtual tours, and take notes on homes they like or wish to pursue further.

Using your agent's portal helps all parties to communicate about specific homes and to stay organized. In addition, agents have access to reports and information that are unavailable on third-party portals such as Zillow and Realtor.com (discussed later). It's far easier to research a property and share relevant information when you're using the same system as your agent.

How much notice do you need for showings?

A successful career agent isn't available to show you a home at the drop of a hat. I schedule my weekend showings three to five days in advance but am often more flexible during the week. In a swift-moving seller's market, acting quickly is often necessary, and I do my best to make myself available. I usually have an assistant who can show a home in case of a scheduling conflict and as a last resort, but I never write an offer on a house I haven't seen in person. Find out how your prospective agent works.

How do you get paid?

Effective August 17, 2024, all Realtors are required to have you sign a Buyer's Representation Agreement before showing you a home. This document describes how the agent gets paid and their rate of compensation. Don't feel pressured into signing a buyer's representation agreement on the spot. Take it home, review it, and negotiate the terms you disagree with. *Buyer Representation Agreements, bonuses, and commissions are discussed in detail later in this chapter.*

How do you work with first-time homebuyers?

First-time homebuyers need – and deserve – extra handholding, education, and care. If you're buying your first home, how will your agent accommodate your need for special attention? I offer "Buyer's Bootcamp" to my first time clients. Our first day together is all about education. Bootcamp helps my buyers clarify their home needs and reduces their fear. They learn to recognize a good house when they see it. What will your agent do for you?

Meaningless Questions

You can ask the following questions, if you like, but don't put too much stock in their answers.

Can you provide a list of your former clients, including their addresses and the amount they saved?

An agent who would give you this information is not very smart – or honest. I would never compromise my client's privacy to get a new client. New homeowners are often targeted by scammers, and I will not inadvertently be part of a transaction that harms my clients. In addition, it's impossible to quantify a buyer's savings or attribute any discount to the agent's skills. Find an agent who has integrity and a genuine concern for things beyond their own financial interests.

How much of a discount can you usually get off the price of a home?

There are far too many variables for anyone to be able to answer this question accurately, and any answer you receive would be a complete guess or an outright lie. Price is only one of many possible seller concessions. In a seller's market when fifteen buyers are competing for the same house, you want the agent who can convince the seller's side to sell the house to you, not one of the other buyers. In the eyes of a seller, my 30 years of working with buyers are far more impressive than an agent with a few transactions under their belt. You need an agent who can present your offer in a way that wins you the house, and often, it has nothing to do with price.

How to Get a Great Agent to Work with You

New agents are so hungry for clients that they will agree to represent almost anyone. They haven't yet learned how to select clients who are ready and able to purchase a home. But an experienced agent is vetting you in the same way you are vetting them. After all, there's no point in representing you if you're not able to close the deal when the right house comes along. And no buyer wants to go through the aggravation and expense of selecting a home, only to learn they can't buy it in the end. They need an honest agent to tell them if a home purchase is out of reach in the short term.

Here are some things agents look for when selecting a client:

- Did the buyer show up on time for their initial meeting?
- Were all parties to the transaction present at the meeting?
- Did they have a general idea where they want to live and what they want to buy?
- Were they fairly open about their financial qualifications?
- Did they have a pre-approval letter from a reputable lender? If not, did they ask for a referral to a lender you like?
- Have they been preparing for a home purchase by saving money for a down payment, monitoring their credit score, or visiting open houses?
- Have they visited my website, so they know a little about me?
- Is buying a house a good move for this buyer? I don't want to be a contributing factor to someone's bad financial decision or

emotional purchase. I'm looking for a level-headed buyer who can make informed decisions.

I carefully select my buyers/clients, but for me, it's more instinctive and practical. Is the potential client ready, willing, and able to buy a home in an area I serve? If so, do I like them enough to have them over for dinner? If the answer is yes—and I have room in my schedule—I'll probably take them on as clients. Sounds crazy, I know. When I commit to representing a buyer, I'm in it for the long haul. I do the same great job for clients I don't click with, but the journey is far more enjoyable when my clients and I like each other as people. Given the choice, I want to work with a buyer who will ultimately become my friend.

How Agents Are Paid

Moehrl v. National Association of Realtors (NAR) was a class-action antitrust lawsuit alleging that the NAR and other large real estate brokerages conspired to inflate commissions by requiring sellers to pay the buyer's broker's commission. The case was filed in 2019 and settled in March 2024, with NAR agreeing to pay $418 million in fines and to implement significant new rules and policy changes. The new rules were rolled out in August 2024 and caused widespread confusion, conflicting narratives, and wild predictions.

With all the hysteria and inaccurate reporting disseminated by the media regarding the NAR lawsuit and how agents are paid, it's essential that we take a deep dive into the topic of agent compensation. In fact, it makes sense to compare what I wrote in the previous version of this book to clarify how agents are paid pre- and post-settlement. Spoiler alert: It's not that different.

Pre-Settlement Compensation (Prior to August 2024)

Here's what I wrote before the lawsuit. "Real estate commissions are generally a seller's expense (which is why the industry is seller-driven). When a homeowner decides to sell their home, they typically hire a traditional Realtor who works with both buyers and sellers. Commissions are negotiable but typically range from 5% to 7% of the home's sale price. Once a listing agreement is signed, the agent lists the home on the MLS and, in doing so, agrees to share the commission with the agent who brings a qualified buyer. At closing, the seller's proceeds are reduced by the negotiated commission.

To illustrate, let's assume an agent takes a listing on a $200,000 house, and the seller agrees to pay a 6% commission to the agents involved in the transaction. The listing broker accepts the 6% commission and agrees to split this payment with the agent/broker who brings the buyer. The house sells for the list price, and the listing broker and the buyer broker each earn half of the commission, or $6,000 each ($200,000 sales price x 0.06 = $12,000/2 = $6,000). "

> *This practice is referred to as a "broker offer of compensation."*

The seller decides the amount each agent will be paid. In the example above, with $12,000 in commissions on the table, the seller might decide to split the commission equally between the buyer's and seller's agents. The seller may offer a flat-fee or no fee to the buyer's agent. The listing agent might agree to list the home for 5% and offer the buyer's agent 3%, keeping 2% for themselves. If a house isn't selling, the listing agent may decide to use part of their own commission to offer a bonus to the buyer's agent to procure a sale, rather than lose the listing if the property doesn't sell. They could choose to offer some agents less than 50%, which often happens when buyers use an online subagent for the seller (and rightfully so). Or, if they can sell the property without a buyer's agent and convince (or sucker) the parties into agreement, they can act as a dual agent or intermediary and keep the full 6% commission, or $12,000, for themselves.

> *Commissions are negotiable between the listing broker and the seller and are set forth in writing in the listing agreement.*

On the buy side, buyers also have the right to interview and negotiate compensation with the agent they chose to represent them. Their agent could be paid an hourly fee, a percentage of the home's sale price, a flat-fee, or any combination of these payment structures. They can be paid by the seller, through broker cooperation, or by the buyer. A buyer's broker may agree to rebate a portion of the negotiated commission to the buyer or keep the entire commission as payment for services. The terms of payment are detailed in a Buyer's Representation Agreement presented to the buyer early in the home-buying process.

Post-Settlement Compensation (After August 2024)

The post-settlement compensation method is the same, but different. Offers of compensation remain, but the *presumptive* offer from the listing broker to the buyer broker no longer exists, and the commission offered to the buyer's agent cannot be posted on the MLS. In other words, as an agent, I can't automatically assume that the seller is willing to pay me as I did in the past. I can't review a listing on the MLS to determine the compensation being offered. Instead, I must call the listing agent to ask what commission, if any, is being offered to the buyer's agent, and whether it will be paid through a broker's offer of compensation, directly by the seller, or by my buyer.

> *Seller agents can (and do) notify buyer agents of the offered commission through email, text, or phone, but not through the MLS.*

Why the change? Listing the buyer's agent's compensation on the MLS made it easy for agents to steer their buyers toward homes that offered higher commissions. Why show a client a property that only pays 2% when the house next door pays 3%? The intent of this change is to "decouple" the selling and buying commissions. Seller's agents negotiate their commission with the seller, and buyer's agents negotiate their commission with their buyer.

In reality, things aren't really that different. The new rules allow for agent compensation to be accomplished in several ways, depending on the brokerage's policies and the parties' preferences, as described below. Note the similarities between the old way of doing business and the new.

Broker Offer of Compensation

This is the default way things have worked for decades and is described in detail in the previous section. When the seller's listing agreement permits "cooperation and compensation," the listing agent takes a listing fee of X% and offers the buyer's agent a portion of the real estate commission for bringing the buyer to the property. Upon closing of the transaction, the commission is disbursed in accordance with the agreement between the respective brokers/agents. On the closing statement, there will be a line item for the commissions of both the listing agent and the buyer agent; the fees are paid from the seller's proceeds at closing. *Buyers don't pay the commission directly out of pocket.*

Buyer's Agent Negotiates Commission with the Seller

Suppose a listing agent or a seller does not *explicitly* offer a commission to the buyer's agent. In this case, the commission becomes a negotiable item, much like the closing date or sales price when an offer is made. The fee is paid out of the seller's proceeds at closing. On the closing statement, there will be a line item for both the listing agent's and the buyer agent's commissions. *Buyers don't pay the commission directly out of pocket.*

Buyer Paid Options

If the seller can't or won't pay the buyer's agent commission, buyers can pay their agent's fee directly. That doesn't mean, necessarily, that the money comes out of pocket. Buyers can work with their lender to cover the cost, roll the commission into the sales price, or pay the fees in cash at closing. This situation may happen when the seller doesn't have enough equity in the property to cover their closing costs. Note: In my 30+ years in real estate, and except for pre-paid, a la carte services, not a single buyer has been required to write me a check for my services.

Summary

Comparing pre-2024 and post-2024 compensation arrangements, you'll notice that very little has changed. Aside from a call or text to the listing agent (if they haven't yet reached out to me), the only change from my perspective is where I add the buyer's agent compensation to the contract: on Page 6 for seller-paid or on Page 12 for broker compensation. Some sellers and listing agents have become more aggressive in negotiating with me to reduce my requested commission, but that's neither new nor a problem; commissions have always been negotiable.

Overall, I think the changes – although minor – have been positive for buyers and sellers alike. Listing agents are now forced to have the hard conversations with their clients about compensation, and to ensure sellers have a clear understanding of how and why real estate commissions are paid from the seller's proceeds. And buyers now have a greater understanding that – even though they don't usually write a check – buyer representation isn't a free service provided to homebuyers. They are also more aware that payment is expected for services rendered, and if the seller is unable or unwilling to cover the buyer's agent commission, the buyer will be responsible for paying their agent.

Representation Agreements

As of August 2024, agents *must* have a written agreement with a buyer (Buyer Representation Agreement) before representing them in a real estate transaction. Most states now permit agents to use a Showing Agreement, which allows them to show a home without representing either party. This section discusses these agreements in detail.

Buyer's Representation Agreement

A buyer's representation agreement is an employment contract that outlines the agent's duties and responsibilities to the buyer and the buyer's duties and responsibilities to the agent.

I've never been a big fan of the standard pre-2024 buyer rep agreement because it generally provided far more protection to the broker than to the buyer. There was nothing that guaranteed the client's satisfaction or protected you from an unskilled or unethical agent. The compensation rates were open-ended rather than capped. They didn't always discuss an agent's duties or responsibilities toward you, even though it demands your loyalty to the brokerage for an extended period, and you were forced to sign at the first meeting with an agent, when you have no way of knowing how responsive or competent they are.

Although these agreements favored the broker, the reasons for having them in place are valid. It's not fair for an agent to spend nights and weekends showing homes, taking calls, conducting research, and interrupting family vacations, only to have their buyer "ghost" them or buy a home through another agent behind their back. Most people don't want to be treated that way. Would you? Buyers shouldn't be able to call a number on a yard sign and have an agent arrive within an hour to show them a home, as if they were ordering a pizza.

> *Buyers need to demonstrate sincerity in their efforts to purchase a home if they want to be taken seriously by real estate agents, who often spend a lot of time with buyers without the guarantee of a paycheck.*

The post-2024 agreements are the same – but different. The same level of protection remains for the broker, but the new agreements are more transparent and fairer to the buyer.

The National Association of Realtors (NAR) now requires that buyer representation agreements clearly state:

- The rate of compensation and who is responsible for payment
- The expectations and duties of each party

- That compensation cannot be open-ended or exceed the rate of compensation listed on the agreement
- That compensation is not set by law

In addition to the requirements of the NAR, every state has its own real estate commission that expands upon these general requirements. Describing them in detail is beyond the scope of this book, but what follows are things to look for in any buyer's representation agreement you are required to sign.

Rate of Compensation

Like any business, real estate brokers establish their own pricing policies, and most brokers allow their agents to do the same. Broker X in Dallas can charge more or less than Broker Y in Fort Worth. An agent who works for broker X can charge more or less than another agent in their office if their broker allows them to set their own commission rates.

The agreement you sign should make clear how much the buyer's agent will be paid. Are they paid a percentage of the sales price? A flat-fee? A combination of both? Is this amount negotiable? What are the terms of the flat-fee, and what services do they provide?

Reality check: Commissions have always been negotiable. Always. If you aren't comfortable with an agent's pricing policies, you can try to negotiate the fee PRIOR to signing the agreement. The agent can accept, counter, or deny your request, just like any other negotiation. If you can't come to terms, you can refuse to sign and find a new agent. If the agent isn't willing to work with the offered commission, they can decline to take you on as a client.

Who is Responsible for Payment

As discussed in a previous section, most buyer's agent commissions will still be paid out of the seller's proceeds at closing, but in the post-lawsuit era, the paperwork will look different. The buyer's representation will describe the payment responsibilities in detail, and you will be required to sign one before you tour homes. What happens if the seller is unable or unwilling to cooperate with buyer agents? Are you expected to pay your agent? (Hint: The answer is yes, if you still want to buy the house.) When does the commission become due and payable? Understand your financial responsibilities before signing any kind of paperwork.

How long does the agreement remain in effect?

Most (if not all) states require a clear start/end date on the agreement. The duration of the agreement is negotiable but is determined by your agent's policies, market conditions, and the type of property you wish to purchase. New construction homes, for example, can take a year to build, so a longer agreement is required. In fast-paced markets, agents might agree to a shorter-term agreement. Regardless of the contract's expiration date, there will always be a protection period to ensure your agent is paid if you buy a home you toured with them.

Is there an "out" clause?

What happens if your agent doesn't live up to the promises they made during your first meeting? Is there a customer satisfaction guarantee and a way out of your contract if you're not happy with the agent's performance? There needs to be. Some agents are better trained to get a buyer under contract than to represent them. If they oversold their qualifications - as real estate agents have been known to do - and you are not happy with their level of knowledge or work ethic, you need a way out!

How are bonuses to the selling agent (BTSA) handled?

It's not uncommon for builders or sellers to offer a bonus to the agent who brings a qualified buyer to the transaction. As a result of the NAR settlement, agents are prohibited from accepting payment from any source that exceeds the compensation rate specified in the buyer's rep agreement without the client's approval.

What does your buyer's agreement say about bonuses? The correct answer should be "all bonuses are passed along to the buyer" at closing. Many agreements state that agents may still accept bonuses if the buyer approves. Are you comfortable with that? You shouldn't be. There shouldn't be a financial incentive for an agent to steer you to a particular home.

Retainers

Some Realtors charge buyers an upfront retainer to screen out time-wasters and collect their gas money in advance. I like the idea of collecting a retainer and have done so in the past, but doing so adds complexity to my bookkeeping, so I no longer bother. If your agent requires a retainer, is it refundable? Under what terms? Who holds the money, and when do you get it back? What if your agent fails to perform? Know the answers to these questions before you write a check.

Negotiate Your Agreement

Don't be afraid to negotiate and dictate the terms of this agreement if you're not comfortable with the terms. Here are some ways you can tweak your contract with your potential agent:

- Instead of committing to a six-month agreement, adopt a one-month agreement with an option to renew later. This will give you time to get to know your agent before making a long-term commitment.
- Have the commitment apply only to the houses that they show you and omit any mention of a time.
- Designate a trial period, after which the full agreement goes into effect unless either party terminates the agreement.

Don't be surprised if you encounter pushback when negotiating. Some agents assume (stupidly) that if you don't want to sign their agreement as-is, you're a time-waster and not a committed buyer. Or they think you're being difficult. If an agent isn't more concerned about your level of comfort than their own, you may wish to find another agent. After all, it's the buyer who assumes all the risk in a transaction. Your needs matter the most.

I personally don't use a long, restrictive buyer's representation agreement. In fact, until the NAR mandated it, I never asked a buyer to sign anything. I'm confident in my skills. If a buyer/client doesn't want to work with me, they are free to go at any time, with no strings attached. Conversely, I want to be able to release a buyer, if necessary, as it sometimes is. Working with me should be the least stressful part of the homebuying process. It's not unreasonable for you to expect the same treatment from the agent you hire.

If It's Not Working Out

If you begin working with an agent and find it's not a good fit, you're not stuck. Don't be intimidated by a wordy buyer representation agreement; you can't be forced to work with an agent you don't like or trust. However, before you fire them, ensure your expectations are reasonable.

Your agent isn't your companion or Uber driver; their job is to help you buy a house, not take you to lunch. Don't expect them to drop everything and show you a house at the last minute. If you need an appointment to get a haircut, you need an appointment to tour homes, but not only because your agent is busy. Many homes are still owner-occupied, and sellers don't have an open-door policy; buyer's agents must schedule appointments and wait for approval before entering the home. You need to arrive on time for all your appointments, as the seller may only allow a 30-minute touring window, and don't expect calls to be returned at all hours of the night. This isn't volunteer work for agents; it's how we support our families and put our kids through college. A new agent anxious to build their career might put up with bad behavior for a while, but an experienced agent will drop you like a bad habit.

If your agent hasn't presented you with houses in a couple of weeks, ask why. Your search criteria may be too narrow, and there may be nothing to show, particularly in low-inventory markets. Agents deserve the opportunity to explain themselves, and it is easier to give them a chance than it is to start over with a new agent. If you have expressed your concerns to the agent and are still unhappy, it's time to fire them.

Firing Your Agent

If your big broker agent has shown you a home you wish to buy, but you have concerns about their skills or level of knowledge, contact their broker (boss) and ask for another agent to be assigned to you. The released agent will be fairly compensated by their broker upon closing.

If you haven't found a house through this agent, review the agreement you signed and determine the terms of the "out" clause. You are usually required to send a written notice terminating the relationship; send the letter to the agent and the agent's broker. If you have a legitimate complaint, speak up and say so! Allegations of fraud and discrimination should always, always, always be reported, and you should never accept substandard treatment of this kind. But if your agent didn't really do anything wrong, and you just lost confidence in them, just politely terminate the relationship. Simply state that your plans have changed and that you wish to terminate the agreement. They can't force you to buy a house through them. In fact, a REALTOR® is not entitled to a commission on a transaction unless they are the "procuring cause" of the sale (i.e., the party who initiated the transaction), regardless of what the agreement states. Brokers won't or can't sue a buyer for terminating the buyer's representation agreement. But if you have an agent show you homes all over town, let them research and negotiate the purchase of a particular home, and later buy the home on your own or with another agent, you will likely be sued and *will most likely lose*! Beware bad real estate karma! You have been warned!

Showing Only Agreements

Some states allow an agent to show homes to a buyer without a buyer's representation agreement if certain conditions are met:

- The agent has not agreed to represent the buyer. If representation is stated *or implied*, a buyer's representation agreement must be used.

- The agent *does not* give advice or opinions about the property. This includes their opinion on the home's price or condition, market conditions, and related factors.
- They don't perform any other real estate brokerage activities, such as running a CMA or providing additional information about the property.

> *The showing agent's job is essentially to open the door to the house and to ensure you don't steal anything. That's it.*

If you like the house they showed you, you must sign a buyer's representation agreement either with the showing agent or with the buyer's agent of your choice to submit an offer.

Why would an agent waste their time showing you a home that they can't help you buy? Because until you have committed to one agent, you're not a buyer. *You're a lead.* Companies like Zillow, Homes.com, and others spend millions of dollars to capture buyer leads and sell them to agents. Since many buyers hire the first agent they meet, regardless of experience or qualifications, agents believe it's worth their time to drop everything to meet a stranger at a home, open the door, and hope to convince them to hire them.

Experienced agents won't work this way. Our time has value, and our safety is paramount. I won't meet a potential client at a property without verifying their identity and confirming their qualifications.

> *Important: Once you sign a buyer's representation agreement and an agent shows you a property, you MUST use them if you decide to purchase the house. No other agent can represent you in the purchase because the original agent is the procuring cause.*

If an agent offers to show you a home and you're not ready to buy or not ready to commit to an agent, don't sign a buyer's representation agreement; sign a showing agreement.

Keeping it Real

Policies, procedures, and rules established by the National Association of Realtors are not always reflective of what's happening in the real world. Let's recap some of these important topics and scenarios and talk about how things work in the day-to-day world of real estate.

Commissions

Have the new rules changed the way agents are paid? No, they haven't. Conversations agents have with their clients have certainly changed, which is a net positive. Seller's agents must field calls and texts from buyer's agents inquiring about compensation and have altered the ways in which they market a property to buyer's agents in their area. The way purchase contracts are written has changed a little, and I have noticed more agents asking me to reduce my commission. Overall, however, there has been very little change in how agents operate. I am still being paid out of the seller's proceeds at closing, not by my buyer, and I am still earning the same commission I have always earned.

Buyer Representation Agreements

Prior to the NAR settlement in August 2024, it wasn't my policy to require buyers to sign a buyer's rep agreement – but I was in the minority. Most big-box brokers required their use and were adamant that brokers like me who didn't were unprofessional. So be it.

My problem isn't with the use of a written agreement between the buyer and the broker; it's with its misuse. It took no time for unscrupulous agents to take advantage of naïve, undereducated buyers who were misguided in their trust. Here's how it happened for two of our buyer/clients.

Prior to coming to us, buyers toured open houses in areas that interested them. The hosting agent would offer to show the buyers additional homes in the neighborhood and would require them, in accordance with state law, to sign a buyer representation agreement. The buyers were told not to worry… the agreement is only effective for one day and only for the houses they toured together.

Little did the buyers know they were now tied to that agent if they wanted to purchase any of the homes they had toured together. When they engaged my company for representation, we were unable to assist them in purchasing those particular homes. Technically, the agent did nothing wrong; they were required to obtain the buyer's signatures on a buyer's rep agreement, and they did so. But they also downplayed the buyer's commitment to the agent. To the buyer, it felt like entrapment.

> *It is vital that you understand the terms and consequences of the agreement you are signing! When you're serious about buying a home, hire an agent first. THEN look at homes. Not serious? Visit open houses or builder's models for fun. Don't sign anything more than a showing agreement.*

As I mentioned in our early discussion of this topic, I'm pleased overall with the outcome of this change and with the use of mandatory buyer rep agreements. It has forced buyers to recognize that agents are professionals who are paid for their services, and that commissions are built into the home's price. The change has also required agents to have dreaded conversations about compensation and types of representation and has sparked discussions about the value they provide to consumers. More transparency can never be a bad thing.

Are Realtor Commissions a Seller's Expense or a Buyer's Expense?

An argument that influenced the filing of the class action lawsuit was that real estate commissions are a seller's expense, since, more often than not, they are paid out of the seller's proceeds at closing.

So, are agent commissions truly a seller's expense? Yes and no. At closing, the seller (usually) GETS a big check. A home purchased 15 years ago for $200,000 with 5% down, for example, may have a current market value of $400,000 and a loan balance of just $135,000, leaving the seller with $265,000 in equity, out of which selling expenses can be paid. Commissions, escrow fees, repairs, title insurance, and other sales expenses reduce the seller's proceeds at closing, but they don't often take money out of the seller's pocket. It simply reduces their net proceeds.

By contrast, the buyer WRITES a big check at closing. When a buyer purchases a home, they need cash for their down payment, inspections, closing costs, appraisal, survey, escrow fees, and more. Asking buyers to pay their agent out of pocket is a significant burden for many, making homeownership even more unaffordable at a time when it's already a challenge to buy a home. *The way agents are paid is based on this premise.*

But I would argue that without the buyer, no one gets paid. When a buyer closes on a home, the seller, agents, title companies, inspectors, surveyors, appraisers, and others all get paid. No buyer? No sale, no closing, and no one gets paid. Therefore, commissions are a buyer's expense.

Regardless of who technically pays the commission, one thing is for certain: Real estate commissions are rolled into the sales price of the home. Except for low-cost MLS listing services, it's still very uncommon for either the buyer or seller to write a check to pay agent's commissions.

CHAPTER TWO

Types of Homes

Although it may seem that sites like Zillow and Realtor.com are an all-inclusive resource for finding a home, that is not the case. This chapter discusses the different types of homes often for sale, as well as where and how to find them.

MLS Listed Homes

The Multiple Listing Service (MLS) is the online database that Realtors use to list and search for homes. Single-family homes, condos, townhomes, land, new construction (partial list), and rental homes are all available on the MLS.

Homes listed on the MLS feed into homebuying portals like Zillow, Realtor.com, Homes.com, and others.

When it comes to finding your dream home, having an agent who leverages technology can make all the difference. Most agents use services that automatically send you new listings via text or email, keeping you informed about what's new on the market in real-time. My online gateway and mobile app allow buyers to sort and categorize listings and communicate with me about the homes that appeal to them. In addition, the MLS provides agents easy access to a wealth of information, from history reports to non-public data shared by the seller and their agent, and it's easy for me to share this important information with my clients when we're all using the same system. I strongly recommend hiring an agent who leverages these technological tools. It not only makes the process easier and more efficient but also more enjoyable.

Do NOT assume that the information listed in the MLS is correct. As with any database, it's garbage in/garbage out. It's very common for agents to import the data from prior MLS listings without verifying its accuracy. You'll often see inaccurate room counts, features, schools, living areas, and room measurements. With so many agents using artificial intelligence (AI) to write property descriptions, the accuracy and usefulness of MLS data are deteriorating rapidly.

Read the information provided in the listing but verify everything. Everything. Every single thing. Most states are "buyer beware" states, meaning it's up to you and your agent to do your due diligence before closing the deal. Sellers and listing agents use disclaimers to protect themselves if they provide inaccurate information, so it's not a problem for them if the information is wrong. But it's a big problem for you.

This is where working with a highly skilled, experienced buyer's agent will be especially helpful. Avoid agents who take a hands-off approach to confirming the accuracy of listing information. You should be working together to verify the square footage, room count, condition, property taxes, HOA dues, and more.

For Sale by Owners (FSBOs)

FSBOs are homes marketed without a listing agent; they are not always listed on the MLS, but your agent can still assist you in purchasing a FSBO.

Homeowners may opt to sell their homes on their own for a variety of reasons:

- The homeowner hates REALTORS®. Can you blame them? We write our job title in all caps with a trademark symbol.
- They believe they can perform much of a listing agent's work on their own without paying an agent.
- It's a strong seller's market, and finding a buyer is almost effortless.
- The homeowners do not have enough equity in the home to pay commissions, so they have no choice but to sell it themselves.

FSBOs have more options than ever when selling their homes. In the past, to get their home listed on the MLS, homeowners had no choice but to hire an agent to represent them and pay a hefty commission. Now, they can pay $100-$500 to have their home listed on the MLS. Once listed, every agent in that area can view the listing and show the home to prospective buyers. The seller offers a commission to the agent who brings the buyer and pays about half of the commission they would normally pay. This can be a very smart way to sell a home, in some cases, IF they make it easy for agents to show the house.

Secret: Realtors hate working with FSBOs

Why? Homeowners often don't know how to value their property, so their homes are often priced incorrectly. I love, love, love negotiating and finding a great FSBO that is priced below market value, and it thrills me when my clients get a great deal. But, more often than not, the house is *way* overpriced, and working with the seller is difficult at best.

I work with FSBOs all the time, but I hate it. Most won't use a lockbox, so the seller must give us access to the property. That means I must schedule an appointment directly with the seller, rather than making a single call to a service that handles all my appointments. That doesn't matter a lot when I'm showing a single home, but that's not usually the case. Fitting the FSBO into the homes on my tour can be challenging since I must accommodate the seller's schedule. Then, when I call the owner to schedule an appointment, they are always suspicious of me and generally grumpy because so many listing agents have contacted them about listing their home. The seller is present for showings and insists on showing us around the house, which is awkward because most buyers feel uncomfortable opening doors and looking in closets when the seller is present. The showing takes three times longer than usual because the seller wants to make small talk and woo the buyers, which throws us off schedule. In addition, the homes are seldom worth considering because they may require an agent's advice on how best to present them to potential buyers. And it's not just about staging. Listing agents ensure the seller provides essential information about the house and are alert to factors that could prevent a successful closing, such as title issues, property defects, and HOA complications. Yes, I hate working with FSBOs. It makes me grumpy just writing about it.

But I'm a professional, so I always look for FSBOs for my clients - but not right away. Once I understand what my buyers hope to buy, I preview the owners' homes and show my clients only the strong possibilities. I always insist on a private showing, so the seller doesn't follow us around while we're there. *Just leave the chocolate chip cookies on the counter and be on your way, pal!*

I run a quick Comparative Market Analysis (CMA) to assess whether the home is priced correctly, and I gather as much information as possible about the seller and the house in case my client decides to make an offer. I need to know that the seller understands how real estate is sold in my state, since I'm not their agent, and it is not my job to help them sell their house. If they make a mistake, I'll catch it. And if it benefits my buyer, I'll use it against them. *That's my job.*

The seller also needs to demonstrate that they know what they are doing, at least at a high level. I will not let my buyers spend a dime until I am convinced that the seller can and will close the deal. The seller has little to lose, monetarily, if a transaction falls apart. My buyer pays earnest and option money and incurs the cost of the inspection and appraisal. They stand to lose several thousand dollars if the seller doesn't close, and it is my job to ensure that doesn't happen.

So, if your agent is not showing you FSBOs, don't assume it's because they are lazy or trying to hide something from you. Sometimes, they are protecting you from a seller who has no idea what they are doing. And if you do end up buying a FSBO, hang on tight. It could be a very bumpy ride!

Third-Party Home Buying Portals

The internet is one of the best tools for buying a home. Websites like Zillow, Trulia, and Realtor.com allow you to search for homes, track interest rates, research schools, and much more. It's important, however, to understand how these sites operate.

Sites like these make money by selling advertising to real estate agents, mortgage companies, insurance agents, and builders. They receive data feeds from Multiple Listing Services nationwide. They massage the data, filter out what they don't like, make it look pretty, and hope you like what you see enough to save the listing and/or contact an agent on their site. When you do, you become a "hot lead." You receive communications from one or multiple agents by phone, text, or email – night and day – until you tell them to stop or until you buy something.

Here are some things you should know about these types of websites:

- The information is often highly inaccurate. Depending on how often they update their database, their home listings can be outdated, with many of the homes already under contract.

- Their home valuations (e.g., Zestimates) are based on the average sales price in a geographic area rather than on comparable sales. Some states (such as Texas) don't allow "sold" data to be made public, so these portals lack the information needed to make such a computation. How can you value a property when you don't know what the houses in the neighborhood sold for? You can't. It's impossible. Automatic valuations are virtually worthless. Ignore them.

- Agents who sign up for their programs are required to respond to your inquiry within minutes. You click "Get More Information," and within a minute, an agent (or five) will call. *You should not hire an agent simply because they were the first to respond to your request to see a home!* The person contacting you is usually an admin or a newly licensed agent paying their dues as part of a real estate team. Remember, any monkey can open the door to a house. Successful agents are busy agents.

- You MUST verify the information listed on these sites. That includes the size, schools, taxes, and history. As previously discussed, the information on the MLS is often highly inaccurate. After these portals revise the data to their liking, it becomes even more questionable. Verify. Verify. Verify.

Online homebuyer portals can help you learn about an area, virtually tour homes, and expedite the homebuying process. My buyers love to view homes across multiple portals, and I have no problem with that. Have fun with these sites. But when you're serious about buying a home, use a platform that makes it easy for you to converse with your agent; that platform provides *direct* access to the Multiple Listing Service.

Instant HomeBuyers (iBuyers)

An iBuyer (Instant HomeBuyer) is a company that uses technology to make instant offers on a home. If you have a home to sell and don't want to list it with a full-service agent, you can sell it to an iBuyer, typically at a significant discount. Open Door, Offer Pad, HomeVestors, and the We Buy Ugly Houses chain are all examples of companies with iBuyer programs. These programs appeal to sellers whose homes need work, are in a rush to sell, are behind on payments, or don't want to go through the hassle of fixing up their homes before listing.

Basically, iBuyers are investors and home flippers. When they purchase a home, they make some improvements to the property, then resell it as quickly as possible and for as much money as possible. When you buy a home from an investor/iBuyer, don't be dazzled by the cosmetic improvements. New flooring, fresh paint, and quartz countertops might make a house look beautiful, but what's happening under the surface? Is the freshly painted brick covering major cracks that indicate a foundation problem? Are the fresh white bathroom tiles new, or were they painted over the old tiles? What shortcuts were taken that may cause you problems later? In some states, homeowners who have not occupied a property can claim they were unaware of the property's history. Even sellers who have owned a property for decades can claim ignorance and decline to share important information that is relevant to the buyer.

> *Since they don't have the same duty to disclose as owner-occupants do, the buyer's risk in purchasing one of these homes is even greater.*

As you would with any home purchase (including new construction), hire a qualified inspector to evaluate the condition of a home you purchase through an iBuyer or any investor. If walls were removed during the remodeling process, hire a structural engineer to ensure the work was performed correctly. Negotiate repairs, and don't be afraid to walk away if the house is a dog.

New Construction

There are some significant advantages to buying a new home. First, there's the "new house smell" and the fact that no one else's feet have ever been on your carpet. More importantly, new homes offer energy-saving features unmatched by homes even just a few years old. They generally include a 10-year transferable structural warranty covering the foundation and load-bearing components, a 2-year systems warranty covering electrical, plumbing, and air conditioning, and a 1-year floor-to-ceiling warranty. However, for every positive, there is a negative, and the negatives range from superficial to deal-killer.

First, you typically pay a high premium for new construction, and (unless you get a *great* deal) it can take about five years before you start to build any equity in your home. Second, builders develop new communities on open land, which generally means longer commutes and greater distance to the center of town and all its amenities. In addition, when the neighborhood is new, you won't know who your neighbors are until after you move in. Does the family next door have six barking dogs and four broken-down cars? It's anybody's guess.

The biggest risk, however, involves the condition of the house. It may take a year or more for defects in the property to become apparent. In my area, the risk is driven by our clay-based soil, which causes frequent foundation problems. In your area, it may be something different, but the assumption that homes are free of problems simply because they are new is wrong, wrong, wrong. Wrong.

Types of New Homes

There are different types of new construction homes. Your budget, time-line, and personal preferences will determine the right type of new home for you. Custom homes, spec homes, and tract homes are discussed below.

Custom Homes

When building a custom home, you make all the choices. You pick the lot, builder, floorplan, architect, faucets, roof, air conditioning, and everything in between. On the plus side, you get *almost* exactly what you want, and you have some control over the price, at least in theory. You move into a home that does not look like every home on the block, and you can take pride in conceptualizing your vision and bringing it to fruition.

Now - the downside. The first obstacle is finding a builder that can deliver everything they promise. You'll worry about the builder going over budget, running off with your money, going bankrupt, whether they can find quality labor to construct your home, and whether your marriage will survive the process. Chances are, they will not finish on time, and ultimately, even with the biggest budget, you will likely get only 95% of what you originally wanted. Theoretically, you could use a Realtor as a second set of eyes and ears, but you probably will not find one dumb enough to get involved. I wouldn't.

Tract Homes

Developers who buy a large parcel of land to divide into smaller lots build what are known as "tract" homes; streets of tract homes create subdivisions. When you think of a tract home, think of David Weekley, Highland Homes, Meritage Homes, Toll Brothers, Ryland Homes, and others. These builders have 8-12 floorplans in a subdivision; they are all similar but not identical. If you're building a tract home from the ground up, you pick a lot, a floorplan, and your cosmetic items (usually), and, if all goes well, eight months later, you have a house.

Because of the volume of homes being built and lower material and labor costs, tract homes are far less expensive than custom homes. Price and availability are the most appealing aspects of tract homes. However, you should know that the quality varies not only by builder, but also by area. Do not assume that Bob's Fancy Homes, for example, builds the same quality product in all parts of town. The price point and their desired profit margin dictate the quality of the materials that they use, and in some areas, the quality is *horrific* (particularly in fast-growing areas). You should also be aware that some builders are far better to work with than others. Some are professional and deliver a quality product on schedule, while others are so poor that I refuse to help a buyer build one of their homes.

If your agent is willing to lose you as a client rather than work with a particular builder, I strongly suggest you heed their advice.

Spec Homes

A spec home (speculative home for sale) is simply a tract home that is built without anyone particular in mind. Spec homes are also known as inventory homes. Builders like to have a few homes ready or nearly ready for buyers who need to move quickly. Sometimes a spec home becomes available when the original buyer backs out of the transaction. And since COVID, we're starting to see more 'spec only' builders, meaning they make all the selections. You accept whatever they pick for you without changes.

The same pros and cons that apply to tract homes also apply to spec homes. You can usually negotiate a far better deal on a spec home than on a build job.

Buying a Tract or Spec Home

Buying a new tract or spec home is *much* different than buying a resale home. First, most builders use their own contract rather than the one promulgated by the real estate commission, and that contract is *not* written to be fair. It is written to benefit the builder, not you!

Next, although this varies by area, most salespeople at a builder's model are not Realtors; they work for the builder and are not licensed or regulated by the state. *That means that they don't have a legal requirement to treat you fairly, and the only knowledge they have about construction and real estate is what they learn in their training classes.* Some builder representatives are better than others, of course. There are some who know a great deal about construction, and others who know a great deal about interior design. The one thing they all have in common, however, is that they want you to buy a house. They don't always care whether you like the house, as long as you close on time and don't say mean things about them online.

Builders welcome, *and usually prefer,* buyers who are represented by an agent; it reduces their liability by making agents responsible for the buyer, allowing them to take a hands-off, buyer-beware approach. Does it cost you more to have representation? Sometimes. Most builders say agent commissions are charged to their marketing budget, so the buyer is not actually paying commissions, and I believe that is true. The vast majority of new construction homes are sold with the help of a real estate agent, so those costs need to be factored into their margins. However, when builders sell spec homes, they sometimes ask potential buyers whether they have an agent before quoting them their best price, and that price *might* be higher if an agent is involved. But don't assume that any money goes into your pocket if you choose not to have representation. It usually doesn't. The builder might make it look like a good deal on the front end, but they'll make it up on the back end, and you'll never know the difference. Or, it's a house they are having a hard time selling, and you'll get stuck with a house no one else wants. Since they can't find any takers, they offer you a great deal to get the house sold; after closing, it's your problem, not theirs.

> *Do not begrudge a Realtor the fee they are paid for their expertise; they are there to help you avoid being ripped off. There is a reason 7 out of 10 new construction homes are sold by Realtors. Without an agent, you'd need a lawyer, and lawyers don't know a lot about buying a home beyond the contracts and title work.*

If you plan to have your agent represent you, be sure to mention them to the salesperson on your first visit (if your agent isn't with you). Or, better yet, give the builder your agent's card and tell him to contact your agent, instead of you, with more information. It will signal that they are not going to be able to rip you off, and it will guarantee that the builder will work with them, since some builders require that your agent be announced on your first visit to their model. The builder's rep will often share information with your agent that they won't share with you about incentives, discounts, etc. If you're working with an Exclusive Buyer's Agent, everything your agent learns about the builder's motivations and bottom line will be shared with you.

What You Should Know About New Construction

Here are some things you should know about buying a spec or building a tract home:

- Builders are most eager to sell their spec homes first because the interest rate on homes under construction (construction financing) is much lower than that on finished, move-in-ready homes (interim financing). It is very expensive for builders to keep homes in inventory. For this reason, spec homes are generally far more negotiable than build jobs, especially if you can close as soon as the house is finished.

- Builders are very reluctant to reduce the sales price, as it risks upsetting other buyers in the neighborhood who might have paid more for their homes. You can generally expect a small price reduction (if any), but more "free" upgrades or incentives, such as tile or quartz.

- Incentives are often used as bait to encourage buyers to make quick decisions. "These incentives apply to these five lots. We have two sold." Or "We're offering a $10,000 decorating allowance through January." If you miss an incentive, don't worry. Your agent can ask the on-site agent to extend it for you, or a new incentive will be available a few days after their current ones expire. It's a game.

- The home you buy will look nothing like the model. Builders often use higher-quality materials in their models and stage them to attract buyers. In fact, there is an entire industry dedicated to the cause! The large primary bedroom you see may appear larger because the room is staged with a shorter, narrower bed than a standard-size bed. I suggest skipping the model walkthrough unless you are looking for decorating ideas. Look at one of their spec homes or a build job nearing completion. Do not be fooled by smoke and mirrors.

- You still need an inspection on a new home. In fact, you need it more since you will be the first person to live in the house. Some buyers opt (at their builder's suggestion) to have their home inspection done a month or two before their one-year warranty ends rather than before closing; I'm not a fan of this strategy, even with top-tier builders. Once you close on a home, you have no leverage if issues arise with the property. What if a shower pan has failed? How will you know if nails caused damage to the roof, and what if it rains before the repair can be made, causing damage to the interior? What if construction debris clogs the a/c drain lines? There are dozens of things that can go wrong and cause damage to the property. Inspection contingencies and inspectors exist for a reason!

- If you are building a home, the salesperson will write the contract to reflect the sale price and include a detailed list of upgrades to be installed. You are often expected to decide which upgrades you want before you go to the design center, or before you know what each item costs. A better way is to negotiate a dollar amount or a budget to use at the design center later.

- When building, insist on a walk-through before the sheetrock goes up to ensure the space between the studs is clean. It is not uncommon for workers to leave trash and food in the empty house and for garbage and sawdust to be left in between the walls.

- Do not ever, ever, ever buy a home from a builder before researching their reputation online, and, as with all reviews, disregard the highs and the lows. And do not be afraid to talk to your neighbors and learn from their experiences. Do this before you sign the contract, since you'll be writing a very large, non-refundable check for your earnest money and paying for some upgrades upfront.

- Most newly constructed homes look great on closing day. Everything is new, shiny, and clean. But how do they look in a year? Is there excessive settlement? Popping tiles? Warped wood? If you're working with an agent, ask them to show you a few resale homes in the neighborhood (assuming you can find any) to see how the houses are holding up to the elements and to normal, day-to-day wear and tear.

- Although new homes come with various warranties, don't assume the builder is going to honor them, even when they use a third-party warranty company. Warranty companies go out of business all the time, and they all have "out" clauses that they can use to get out of fixing your house. Do your due diligence in advance by getting the necessary inspections and hope you get lucky when you file a warranty claim.

- Builders usually have preferred lenders and title companies. They will often offer you $10,000 in closing costs, for example, if you use their preferred lender. They claim their rates are competitive, but you must shop around to be sure. It's all about the math. The cheapest loan, after factoring in the builder's contribution to your closing costs, gets your business (assuming they can close on time). Cost means total cost, not upfront cost. You are losing money if the builder gives you $10,000 in closing costs but offers you a 6.5 percent interest rate, when you can get 6.00 percent or less through another mortgage company. In the long run, you will save a lot more than $10,000 when you get a loan with a lower interest rate. Shop around and do the math. And you shouldn't feel bad about switching TO the builder's lender if your current one can't meet or beat their deal. I've had many buyers who feel guilty for not using the lender who spent a lot of time getting them pre-approved. Don't. Send them a thank you gift card or leave them a nice review if it makes you feel better. But do what's best for you.

- Builders also offer incentives to use their affiliated title company. Often, the incentive is a "free" title policy. If the title incentive is separate from the mortgage incentive, it can be a pretty good deal. If not, it is, once again, all about the math.

- Don't expect to close on time! Things go wrong with new construction. Weather delays, labor issues, supply chain problems, and other factors can push back the builder's anticipated closing date. Don't schedule a moving truck or move out of your current residence until you are absolutely certain that closing will happen. And, even then, it never hurts to pad your moving day by a week, just in case.

I understand the allure of buying a new home. Have a good agent represent you, do your research, do the math, and hope for the best. Remember that any stress or frustration you feel will ease once you move into your beautiful new home.

Foreclosures and Short Sales

When a homeowner stops making their mortgage payments, the bank repossesses the property through a process called foreclosure. A short sale is a sale of a house for less than the balance on its mortgage. If, for example, the seller has a mortgage balance of $300,000 but can only net $275,000 from the sale proceeds, the bank might agree to reduce the outstanding balance to avoid the costly foreclosure process.

The techniques used to buy a property that has been foreclosed upon and the risks involved in doing so are beyond the scope of this book. But my experience working with foreclosures has shown me that it is difficult to make the numbers work, particularly in a seller's market.

Let's say a bank-owned property (foreclosure) interests you, and the sales price is $400,000. You estimate the home needs approximately $50,000 in repairs and improvements. Your agent analyzes the market and determines that similar-sized, well-maintained homes sell for an average of $475,000. Assuming there are no surprises, you fix up the house and net $25,000 in equity. Is $25,000 enough to justify the substantial risk and effort involved with buying properties that are typically in poor condition? To some, it is, particularly buyers who plan to live in the home rather than resell it for a profit right away. It was to me when I first started flipping homes. I soon realized I was earning below minimum wage for my efforts and learned that I had to buy homes much cheaper if I was going to make money as a flipper.

It is very difficult, in my opinion, and in this market, to buy a foreclosed house cheap enough to make it worth the trouble and to justify the risk. The only exception I have found involves very high-end luxury homes. So, if you are in the market for a luxury home, keep your eyes open for a good foreclosure. Otherwise - buyer beware. And be sure to hire an agent with extensive experience handling foreclosures. It's a specialty, for sure.

Short sales are sometimes referred to as pre-foreclosures and can be worth pursuing under certain circumstances. The problem, however, is that the bank may take several weeks or even months to approve the contract. It can sometimes take up to a year to close! If you are looking at short sales, focus on those that already have bank approval and save yourself months of wondering whether you can buy a particular house. It's just not wise to tie your money up that way.

CHAPTER THREE

The Right House for You

When shopping for a home, there are many factors to consider, like location, budget, property condition, school districts, resale value, floor plan, and the potential for appreciation versus depreciation. It's helpful to begin by listing the features that matter to you, then rank them in order of importance. Doing this before you start viewing homes will help you stay focused and avoid distractions, such as décor and cosmetic updates. The following are things to consider before you begin your home search.

Price Range

A quick call to a lender will help you determine your buying power, the cash you'll need to close, and suitable loan programs. It's important to understand that there is a significant difference between the amount of money the bank will lend you, what you can truly afford, and what you should be willing to spend.

Just because the bank is willing to lend you $800,000 doesn't mean it's a good idea to borrow that much! Remember that lenders get paid based on the loan amount; the more you borrow, the higher their profits.

Set a budget and stick to it. Consider the monthly cost of utilities, repairs, cleaning, maintenance, and furniture. You'll want money to save for retirement and to fund your children's education. Aim to buy everything you need, but just some of what you want. There is a difference.

If you're in the early stages of the homebuying process, pre-qualifying through a lender - even an online lender - is a sufficient and beneficial step. This process is simple. You provide the lender with your overall financial picture that includes your debt, income, and assets, and agree to a soft credit check that won't affect your credit score. You don't need to send financial documents or sign anything. Just fill out the application. After evaluating this information, the lender will provide an estimate of the mortgage amount you qualify for and the cash you will need at closing. While a pre-qualification is not enough to submit an offer, it will give you a clear picture of the amount you can (probably) qualify for and help you determine a comfortable price range. There is more – much more – about mortgages later.

*Don't use an online calculator to determine what you can afford! Talk to an actual lender who can accurately calculate your **allowable** income and provide realistic qualifying ratios and rates.*

Bedrooms and Bathrooms

The most practical and flexible single family home has at least four bedrooms or three bedrooms plus a study. For resale purposes, anyone who can fit into a three-bedroom home can easily fit into a four-bedroom, but the opposite is not true. A family needing four bedrooms would never consider a home with only three. If a four-bedroom home is outside your budget, don't worry about it. But be mindful of the shared living space's size and functionality and ensure there is an area for a home office, as this is a "must-have" for many homebuyers these days. Tell your agent you'd like a three-bedroom home with a study, or a space that can be used as a study, such as a formal living room.

One Story or Two Story Home

There are advantages and disadvantages to both one-story and two-story homes.

In a one-story house, ceilings are higher, and there is no noise from people walking overhead. It is easier and safer for small children, the elderly, or the disabled to live on one floor, and you don't have wasted space where the stairs would go. On the downside, the yard is typically smaller due to the house's larger footprint. There is typically less privacy, and the bedrooms are often smaller.

Living in a two-story home usually means better views from the second floor and more separation between living spaces and bedrooms. It can feel safer to leave windows open on the second floor since it's harder for the boogie man to climb through a second-story window. The yard is often larger, and if you have zoned heating/cooling, you won't have to heat or cool the first floor while sleeping (assuming all bedrooms are upstairs). On the downside, people walking on the second floor can generate a lot of noise, particularly in lower-end homes with lower-quality materials. In addition, stairs can be inconvenient or prohibitive if a family member becomes injured or sick.

Living Areas

A living area is a visually and functionally distinct area within the home intended for general use, versus a bathroom, kitchen, or sleeping area, which serves a specific purpose. A *formal* living room is typically located at the front of the house and used for special occasions or entertaining. Furnishings are typically more upscale and arranged for conversation rather than watching television. Since today's families tend to live more informally than in years past, many buyers prefer not to have a formal living area, opting instead for more functional, usable spaces such as a home office or a game room.

The *family* room is typically where everyone gathers to watch television or just hang out, so make sure this space is on the larger side and be mindful of traffic patterns once all your furniture is in place. You'll need a 3' wide walkway to move from one space to the next. If you have children and want them to have a separate space for their toys and friends, be sure to find a home with at least two living areas or a spare bedroom to use for this purpose. Many people like having an upstairs game room for the kids and their mess. This feature is particularly useful for older children, since they enjoy their solitude and privacy.

Dining Areas

Although it's common for college students, teens, single adults, and empty nesters to eat their meals on the couch in front of the TV (guilty as charged), most civilized people eat in the breakfast room or formal dining room (on special occasions). The breakfast room should be large enough to comfortably accommodate a table and *at least* four chairs. If the door to the backyard is adjacent to the breakfast room, verify there is sufficient clearance for the door to operate properly after the dinette is in place. Formal dining rooms should be large enough to accommodate at least six chairs.

Builders of more moderate priced homes are now eliminating formal dining rooms and replacing them with luxurious home offices or flex spaces. If you buy a home without a formal dining room, ensure the breakfast room is large enough to accommodate a larger table and at least six chairs, since this space will be used for both daily meals and special occasions. If you buy a home with two dining rooms, the formal dining room should be close to the kitchen to make serving more efficient.

Garage Space

Buying a house with a garage is generally a good idea, as it provides valuable storage space, protects your vehicle from the elements, enhances security, and can significantly increase your home's resale value, especially if you live in an area with harsh weather.

In many parts of the country, it's common for homes to have at least a two car garage, the minimum size to fit two cars being 20'x20'. If you drive an SUV or truck, be mindful of the garage door height, as clearance can be an issue. More space is better than less, since you'll also need room for lawn equipment, tools, and other items.

If you are purchasing a home in a neighborhood where most homes have a three car garage, try to buy a house with the same. You want your house to blend with the other homes in the neighborhood.

Occasionally, you may encounter homes where the homeowners have converted the garage into living space. Ensure the space can easily be converted back to a garage, as homes without a garage can be challenging to sell.

Square Feet

Many Realtors recommend an ideal square footage of about 600–700 per person. That means a family of three will want a house that's at least 1,800 square feet, a family of four will want a home that's around 2,400 square feet, etc. Take this advice with a grain of salt, since a person's need for personal space varies widely based on how they grew up, their culture, how many things they own, and how much they enjoy their spouse and kids.

When house hunting, it's wise to have a general idea of what 3,000 square feet looks and feels like, but don't get too concerned with exact numbers. The floor plan and room count matter more than a house's square footage. A well-designed floor plan can make a 2,500 square foot home feel like a palace. Conversely, a 4,000 square foot home can feel small if there is insufficient usable space or the design is poor.

If you think you need a 3,000 square foot home, let your agent show you homes in the 2,700 to 3,300 square foot range. Consider homes that are slightly larger and slightly smaller. You never know when a house you tour will be the house, even though it isn't perfect on paper.

Age of Home

If you are concerned about energy conservation and your utility bills, newer is better - by far. The cost to cool a home built in the 1980s can be triple that of a similarly sized home built in 2000 or later. Improvements in insulation, windows, roof decking/radiant barriers, appliances, and HVAC systems have *substantially* reduced the cost of heating and cooling a home.

Sacrifices are to be made, however. Older homes were typically built on larger, sometimes more beautiful lots, with a very different look and feel from new homes (for better or worse). If you are unsure of your preference, let your agent show you a few older homes. You will know right away if older homes are something you wish to consider. An older home, beautifully updated and on a large, beautiful lot, could be the answer for you.

Area

The area where you plan to buy is a hugely important decision and not one to be taken lightly. How far are you willing to drive to get to work? Do you want to be close to downtown, or are you happy in the suburbs? Schools are always important to consider, and you should buy a home in a decent school district, even if you don't have children. Find out where the good schools are and then take a ride to that area. Or go online, find some homes in your price range, and drive around those neighborhoods to see how you like them. An afternoon in the car can answer a lot of your questions. What feels like home to you? You're the only one who can answer that question.

Federal, state, and local laws prohibit real estate agents from steering homebuyers to communities based on race or ethnicity. Agents can't tell you which neighborhoods are "good," where to send your kids to school, or where the purple people live. However, they can provide resources such as school district boundaries and phone numbers for the local police department for crime statistics, and a list of nearby places of worship. But they can't and won't tell you where to live. You'll need to do this legwork on your own.

Yard Size

What is your yard requirement? Mine is complete privacy. I don't want to see my neighbors, and I don't want them to see me since coffee outside in my PJs is my daily ritual. Do you want a small yard with minimal maintenance? Are you a gardener? Do you have pets or kids that need room to run? Will the two-story home behind you interfere with your enjoyment of the backyard? You decide.

Most buyers generally look for a home with at least a little outdoor space and some privacy. Buying a home without a small grassy area for a pet is a mistake, even when there's a backyard pool. And, unless you are buying a townhouse, don't buy a house with the smallest yard in the neighborhood; you may have a hard time selling when the time comes. Play the averages and find a home with an average-sized lot or larger.

Remember that a large yard requires more maintenance and a higher water bill. If you are unwilling to do the work yourself, ensure you have the money to hire someone. The fastest way to be the most hated person in the neighborhood is to neglect your outdoor space.

Property Condition & Updates

Unless you're moving into a new, customized house, there's a good chance you'll make at least minor renovations to any home you buy. In many cases, even if a kitchen or living room doesn't feel dated, you may want to paint walls, replace flooring, or refinish cabinets, for example. Putting your stamp on a home is part of the fun of home ownership!

But what about the more significant improvements? Do you have the budget to update an HVAC, plumbing, or electrical system? Do you have the time, money, and patience to deal with contractors? If you plan to do the work yourself, you should know that improvements - even painting - are not as easy as they make it look on HGTV. Have plenty of "oops" money set aside, just in case.

Swimming Pool

People don't always realize the work, money, and stress of owning and maintaining a pool. The cost of cleaning, heating, water, chemicals, insurance, and equipment is high. There is constant concern about the safety of your children, pets, and even the neighborhood children since drowning is the leading cause of death in children under the age of four.

On the other hand, pools are a lot of fun, particularly if you live in an area where you can enjoy them throughout the year. Beyond offering a personal oasis for relaxation, a pool can provide a convenient setting for fitness and become the heart of your social life.

If you are not 100% certain that you want a pool, you shouldn't own one. However, if you know you want one, buying a home with an in-ground pool already installed is preferable. If you add a pool later, you will only recoup about 50 percent of your original cost when you sell the home.

Basements

Basements are the norm in many parts of the country, particularly in the Midwest and Northeast, where soil conditions are stable, and water tables are accommodating. A finished basement can substantially increase your livable space and serve as a game room, extra bedroom, home office, or additional storage. On the downside, basements are the lowest points in the house and are prone to flooding. If not maintained, they can develop a musty odor, and mold can grow. Even though basement risks are relatively low, if most homes in your area have one, you need one, too. Otherwise, you'll take a hit when it is time to sell.

Exposure

The direction a house faces is called its "exposure" and is a matter of personal preference. In some cultures, an east-facing home is considered lucky. If the front of a house faces north, the backyard has more sun in the summer. Homes facing south generally receive afternoon shade in the backyard, which is desirable in warmer climates. The floor plan and location of the rooms will determine the home's comfort level, so unless your concerns are cultural or religious, don't eliminate homes based on exposure before you see the layout.

Nuisance Factors

When touring a home, listen for things that may annoy you, like barking dogs, traffic from local schools or retail establishments, airplanes, trains, and noise from distant freeways. Remember, even if it doesn't bother you during the day when there is a lot of activity in the house, the noise may annoy you at night. It's prudent to visit the neighborhood at different times of day and evening to see what you can see and hear what you can hear. Better safe than sorry!

Resale Potential

The secret to buying a home with strong resale potential is to buy one that attracts the largest pool of buyers. That means none of the following: homes in bad locations, such as next to busy streets, schools, commercial property, or power lines; homes without ample parking, a pantry, or linen closet; homes that have the smallest yard in the neighborhood; homes without a basement or garage when the vast majority of homes in the area have basements and garages; homes with unlivable floorplans; and homes with small closets and inadequate storage. The owners of these homes will try to distract you with beautiful landscaping, hardwood floors, and stainless steel appliances. Don't be the buyer of someone else's problem. Just don't!

Floor Plans

An ideal floor plan ensures smooth traffic flow throughout the house. You need the right number of rooms and a place for everyone in the family to work, play, and sleep. You also need a well-placed kitchen near the family room, easy access to the laundry room, and plenty of storage.

How does the layout support or hinder your daily routine? Is it easy to get the groceries from the garage to the kitchen? Are quiet spaces like bedrooms far enough away from public spaces like the kitchen and living room? Is there a large pantry for storing food and a place for supplies in the laundry room? Is there a lot of wasted space that seems to serve no purpose?

What follows are some general rules that apply to many people.

Kitchen

An ideal floor plan is one in which the garage opens into the utility room, which leads to the kitchen, so you don't have to carry your groceries from the garage across the house to the kitchen, as in Figure 1 (below).

Figure 1: Garage Far From Kitchen

The kitchen layout determines the space's functionality and comfort. The layout shouldn't be confused with an open concept kitchen; open concept simply refers to the lack of walls between the kitchen and family room, while the layout refers to the placement of cabinets, countertops, and appliances. Common kitchen layouts include:

- U-Shaped Kitchen – This layout forms a U-shape, with three walls of cabinets and appliances. It provides plenty of storage and counter space.
- L-Shaped Kitchen – An L-shaped kitchen has adjoining walls forming an L-shape. Compared to the U-shape, counter space is limited. This plan is best for small kitchens.
- Galley Kitchen – A galley kitchen has two parallel walls with a narrow walkway in between. This plan can feel cramped and provides limited storage and counter space.
- Island Kitchen – Usually seen in larger kitchens, this plan has a multipurpose island in the middle of the space. It provides extra storage and workspace and is great for entertaining.
- Single Wall Kitchens – Seen in studio apartments and tiny homes, this layout aligns all the cabinets, appliances, and countertops on a single wall.

Open Concept Kitchen

An open concept kitchen (Figure 2) is one in which the kitchen, breakfast room, and family room function as a single, continuous space rather than smaller, sectioned areas. Without walls and barriers, a spacious, interactive great room is created. An open concept kitchen has several advantages:

- Cooks can interact with family or guests in the living area.
- Young children can be supervised while meals are being prepared.

- Without walls, natural light can more easily spread throughout the home, making the space feel larger.
- The space has a seamless, modern, airy feel.
- Islands and peninsulas serve as prep areas, dining spots or homework hubs.

While there are many advantages to an open concept kitchen, it's not all rainbows and butterflies. Here are some disadvantages:

- Cooking sounds and smells spread through the entire living space, so high-quality, quiet appliances are required along with robust ventilation systems.
- Messy countertops are visible from the living room, so strict cleaning routines are required.
- Removing walls can mean less wall space for upper cabinets, reducing storage.

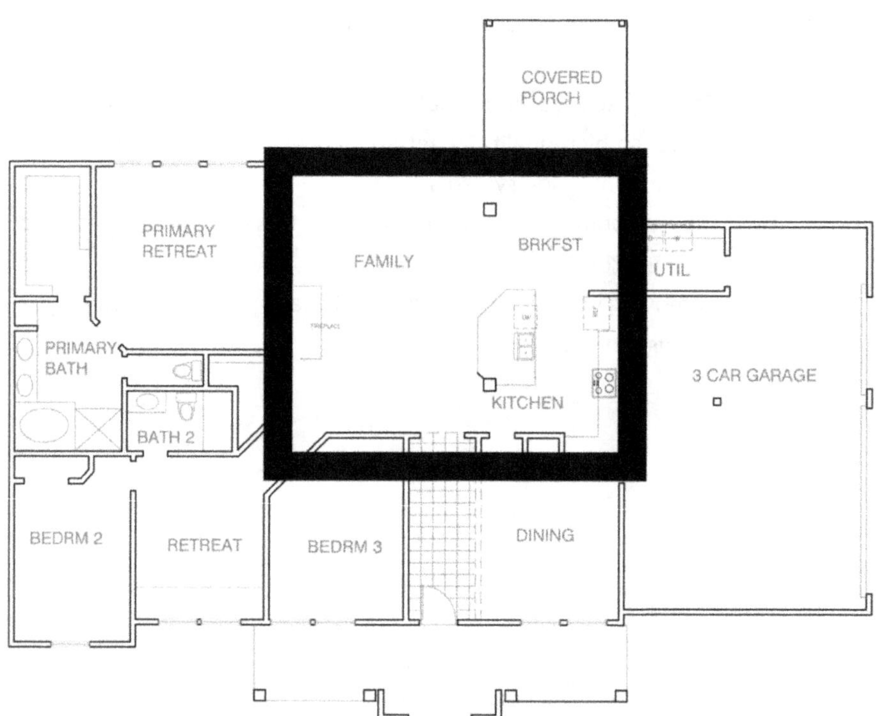

Figure 2: Open Concept Kitchen

Formal Living & Dining Combo (Stacked)

In a stacked or combo plan (Figure 3), the formal living and dining rooms are combined into a single large space that occupies much of the front of the house, leaving a significant amount of unused space. Because the space is open, most people won't use this space as an office or for any other purpose. So, unless you're buying a large home with plenty of extra rooms, this plan may not be the best choice in terms of usability and functionality. Many buyers are initially attracted to this plan. You open the front door, walk inside, and the first thing you see is a bright, airy open space. But after some reflection and analysis, they realize that a house with this plan isn't the way to go. In fact, most builders have stopped building homes with this setup altogether due to lack of demand.

In some cases, it is possible to enclose the living space to create a private office rather than a formal living room. A little sheetrock and French doors are all you need to transform this space from unusable to the highly functional office of your dreams!

Formal Living & Dining Split

A split formal floor plan (Figure 4) has the dining room on one side of the front door and the formal living room on the other. Adding French doors to the formal living room will transform it into a home office, nursery, or play area. This plan is far more flexible, functional, and practical than a stacked-formal plan, and will appeal to far more buyers when it's time to sell your home. Some builders refer to the formal living room in this plan as "flex space."

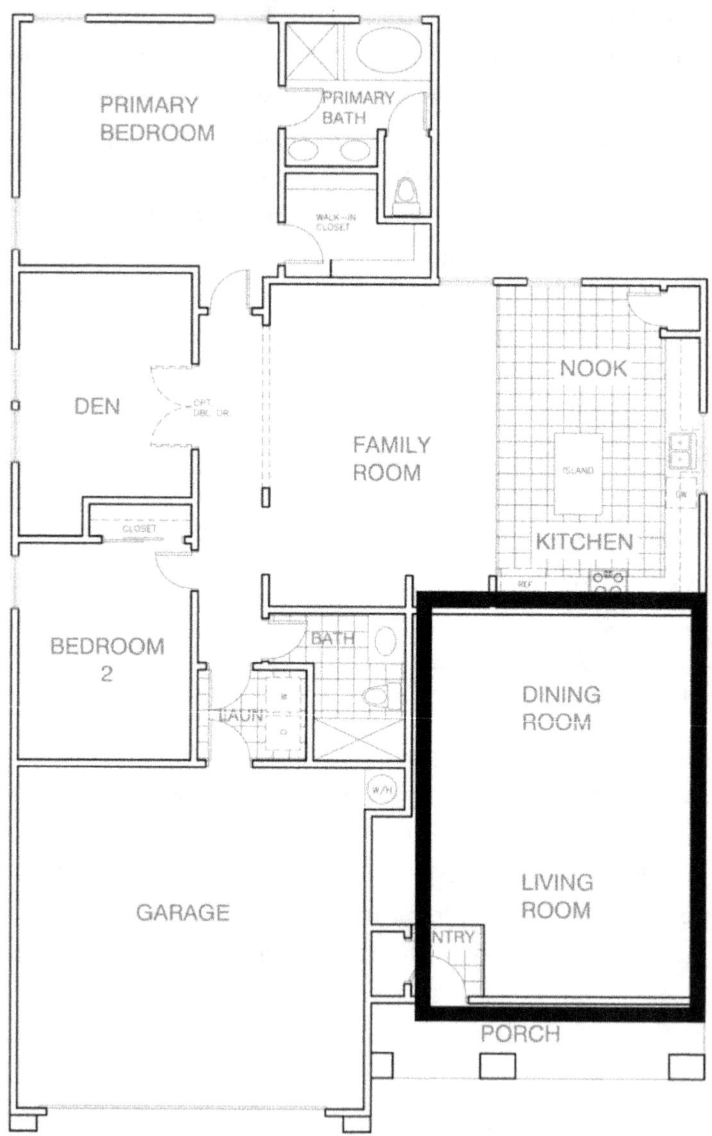

Figure 3: Stacked Formals

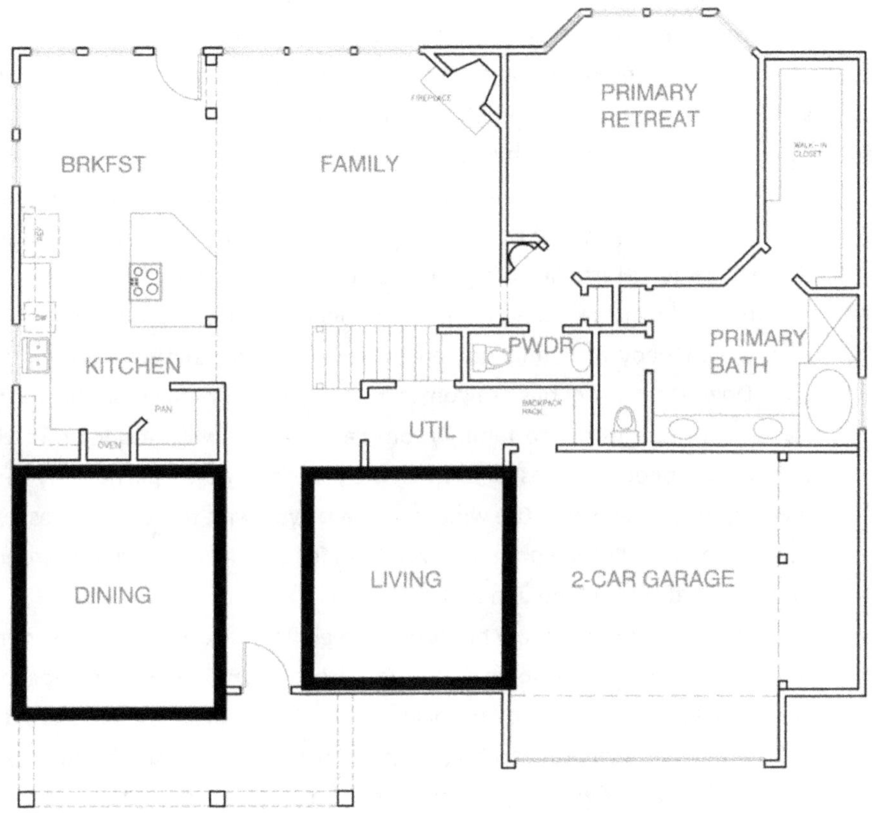

Figure 4: Split Formals

Primary Bedrooms

Many newer homes have the primary bedroom on the first floor and the secondary bedrooms upstairs. The benefits are obvious. Not only do adults have private space away from children, but children also feel more independent when parents aren't hovering nearby. A downstairs primary allows parents to "age in place" because they won't have to relocate when climbing stairs becomes cumbersome. If someone is injured or elderly parents come to visit, there is always a convenient, safe place for them to sleep. Homes with a downstairs primary sell more quickly (in many areas) than those without. There are many good reasons to buy a home with the primary bedroom downstairs, long-term flexibility and resale value among them.

On the downside, some buyers have learned that it is inconvenient to have a new baby or young kids on the second floor, away from their parents. Downstairs primaries are sometimes smaller than those on the second floor, and noise from the family room can interfere with a person resting nearby. And people feel less safe when the primary is down, particularly when it comes to sleeping with the windows open. Even with these negatives, I receive far more calls for a primary down than for one up, although preferences and standards vary by person and area.

In addition to the primary bedroom's level (first or second floor), be mindful of the location of the downstairs primary bedroom. The preferred location is in the back of the house overlooking the backyard. Ideally, there should be at least a small hallway separating the primary bedroom from the family room (Figure 5). In other words, you should not be able to see inside the primary bedroom from the family room.

Primary bedrooms located in the front of the house are not nearly as desirable as those located in the back (Figure 6). Though not necessarily a deal killer, you will lose a few buyers when it is time to resell.

An ideal and highly sought-after floor plan has both the master and a second bedroom downstairs, and two or three bedrooms upstairs (Figure 6). The pictured plan would be better, however, if bedroom 5 were located away from the master bedroom so that all occupants have more privacy.

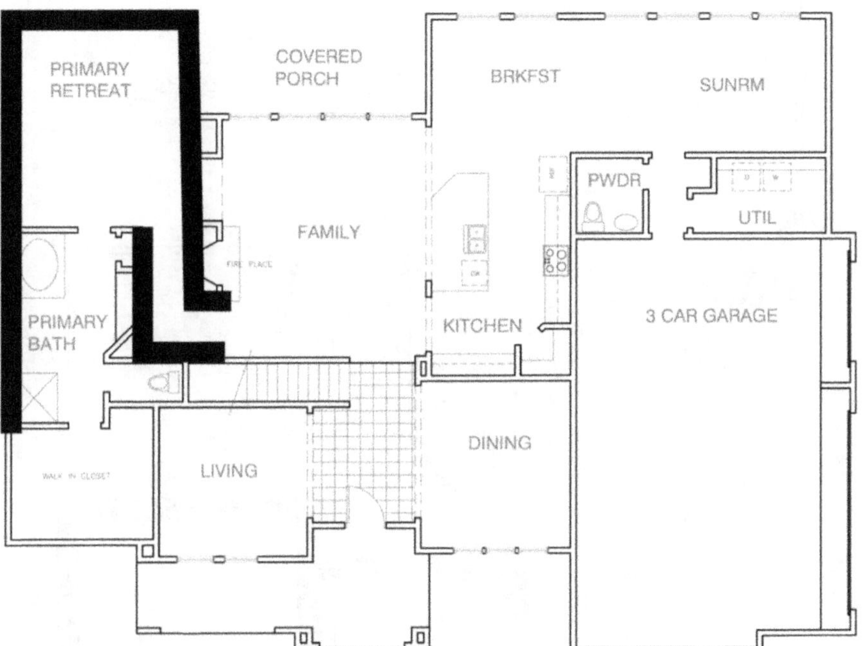

Figure 5: Primary in Back

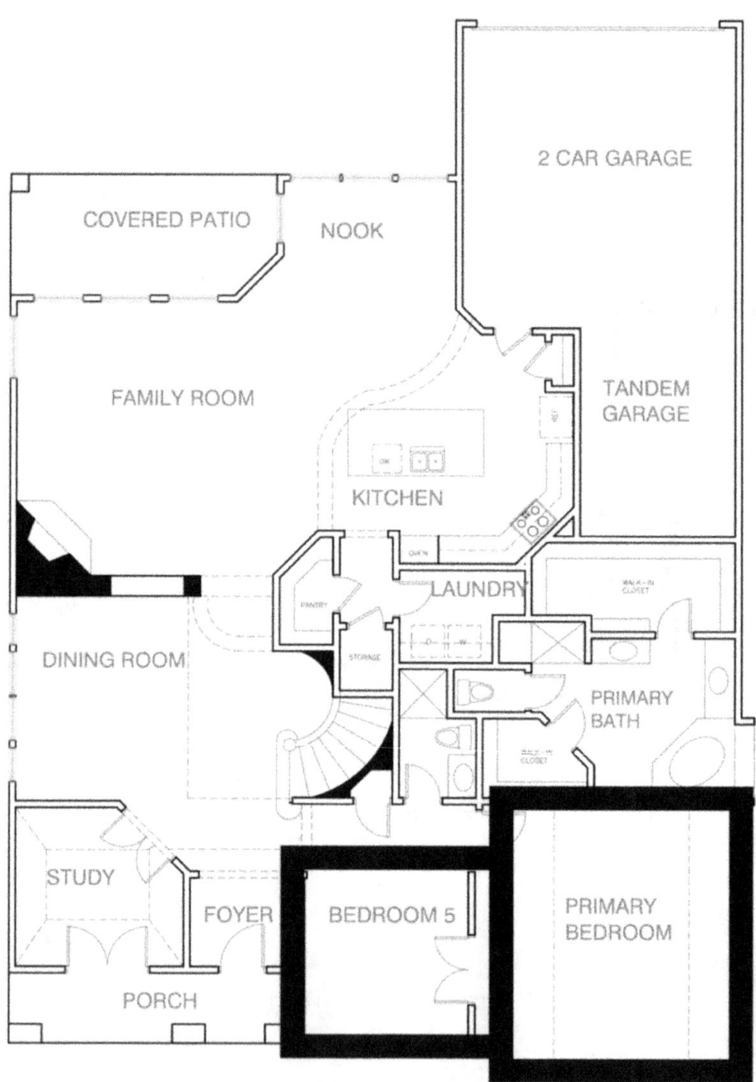

Figure 6: Primary and Second Bdrm in Front

Split Bedrooms

In single-story homes, a three-way split allows family members some privacy. As shown in Figure 7 below, bedrooms are located on opposite sides of the home, separated by the family room.

Figure 7: Three Way Split

CHAPTER FOUR

Due Diligence

Due diligence is the process every buyer must go through – *before* finalizing a home purchase – to ensure your investment makes practical and financial sense, and to uncover any deficiency with the property. In other words, it's the time you take to verify *everything* before you commit to *anything*. Your due diligence or option *period* is the time you have to hire an inspector, negotiate repairs, confirm a clear title, review HOA restrictions, confirm your financing, and more. This chapter takes a deep dive into these items.

Property Condition

Real estate agents are not inspectors, but a good agent should be able to identify obvious issues, like damaged roofs and foundation problems. I stand behind my commitment to protect my buyers, and your agent should too. If my buyers' inspection reveals major concerns that I missed, and they choose not to move forward with the purchase, I will reimburse them for the cost of their next home inspection. My job isn't to sell them a house — it's to help them buy the right one. It's not unreasonable to expect the agent you hire to have the same level of knowledge and confidence in their skill set.

The seller is required to disclose all known defects in the property. Do they? No, they don't. Some sellers withhold information and claim ignorance; others are sincere when they say they are unaware of the condition of certain things. As a buyer, you're entitled to know the age and condition of the roof, foundation, HVAC, plumbing, electrical system, windows, appliances, and more before you finalize the sale, but since you can't count on the seller to provide you with this information, you'll need to figure it out for yourself (with the help of your agent and inspector).

The following provides general guidelines for evaluating a property. Any decent inspector should be skilled at identifying issues with these elements, but it helps to have a general understanding of the property's condition when deciding how much to offer for a home. Note that different materials are used across the country; this discussion is not all-inclusive.

Roof

There are many types of roofing materials, including asphalt composite shingles, metal shingles, wood shakes, slate, and clay tile. Asphalt shingles are the most popular and common choice due to their low cost and long lifespan. When comparing asphalt shingles, know that an "architectural" or "dimensional" shingle is far better than a "3-tab" shingle. Not only do architectural shingles look better, but they also last longer and withstand high winds and hail far better than a 3-tab shingle.

If an asphalt roof is more than 20 years old, it is likely nearing the end of its lifespan, but newer roofs can have issues as well. Look for shingles that are lifting, cracked, curled, or missing altogether, and note areas where the granules have worn off. In areas with frequent hail, look for dents or dings in the shingles to identify damage. Also, look for water stains on the underside of the roof and on the ceiling.

Remember that the roof MUST be insurable for you to buy the home; your financing depends on it. If the roof is damaged by wind or hail, ask the seller to file a claim with their insurance company and have a new roof installed BEFORE you close. Be sure to specify the type of roof and the shingles you want. Don't let the seller replace an architectural shingle roof with a cheap, 3-tab roof to save money.

Most insurance companies don't inspect the property until after closing; the last thing you want is for your policy to be cancelled after closing, when it's too late to negotiate with the seller. This repair or replacement cannot wait until after closing (unless you're paying cash for the property and don't care about having hazard insurance).

Foundation

Foundation problems are usually caused by lousy drainage, bad soil, ground movement, or poor construction, which can cause the foundation to shift or settle. Signs of foundation problems include:

- Doors and windows that no longer open or close.
- Drywall cracks.
- Cracks in the slab and bricks.
- Slab cracks visible on vinyl floors
- Cracked tiles that don't lie flat
- Slanted floors

If you suspect a house might have a foundation issue, or if the seller has disclosed a foundation repair or settlement, hire a structural engineer to evaluate the property. *Consider this a non-negotiable!* Insist that the seller make the recommended repairs prior to closing, and don't spend your own money repairing a home you don't yet own. Lifting a home to level its foundation can cause plumbing issues and leaks under the house. Let the seller assume that risk, not you.

Should you ever consider a home that has already had a foundation repair? Maybe. It might be acceptable if the repair was successful, relatively minor, and included a lifetime, transferable warranty. Find out who made the repair and ensure they are still in business before counting on a warranty. And rely on the opinion of a structural engineer, not the seller's word or a foundation repair company. Foundation repair providers are not licensed in most states. Their goal is to sell you an expensive foundation repair. Please don't count on them for unbiased advice; hire an engineer.

Sprinkler System

If you've ever lived in a property with a sprinkler system, it will be hard for you to imagine life without one. An automatic sprinkler system not only saves you time and effort but also conserves water, increases your home's value, and helps you maintain a healthy, vibrant yard and landscape. And in areas prone to dry soil and foundation problems, a drip line – whether manual or automatic – is an invaluable asset. A sprinkler drip line is a system of tubing that slowly drips water along the perimeter of a home's foundation to maintain consistent moisture levels in the soil. This is crucial during dry periods to prevent soil shrinkage and the resulting foundation cracks, uneven floors, or other structural damage. It is an efficient, effective watering method that minimizes overspray and evaporation compared with traditional sprinklers.

When buying a home with a sprinkler system, be sure to have it inspected during your regular home inspection. It is common for sprinkler heads to break, usually when someone runs over them with the lawn mower; these are cheap and easy to repair. An underground leak, however, can be labor-intensive and costly to fix. This is something the seller should fix for you prior to closing. You should also pay attention to the location of sprinkler heads so you know what you are buying. Some homes only have sprinklers installed in the front or back, not the sides. You want to avoid overpaying for the house because you assumed the yard is fully sprinklered when, in fact, it only offers partial coverage.

Air Conditioners and Heaters

It is important that you know the age and general condition of the HVAC *before* you make an offer. Look at both the inside unit (the air handler, furnace if it also heats, or the evaporator) and the outside unit (the condenser) and note any dust or rust. Try to find a tag that lists the year the unit was manufactured. Improper maintenance will significantly shorten the life of heating and cooling systems. If the units are very old or appear neglected, be sure to factor in replacement costs when making your offer.

> *It is crucial that the condenser (outdoor unit) and evaporator coil (indoor unit) are matched in capacity, efficiency, and refrigerant type! Know what you're buying.*

Your inspector will test the heater and air conditioner to verify operability and age, but they can't open the units, inspect the coils, or provide the level of detail a licensed HVAC professional will. If you have concerns about the cooling or heating system, hire an expert to provide unbiased feedback. Alternatively, if your inspector identifies a problem with the system, ask the seller to hire an HVAC specialist to make all necessary repairs before closing. Talk to your agent about the best course of action.

Windows

Good windows are crucial for energy efficiency, security, and curb appeal, so look for features such as double- or triple-pane glass, low-E coatings, proper seals, and frame materials (vinyl, fiberglass) suited to your climate.

The most common problems with home windows are drafts and air leaks, condensation/fogging between panes, difficulty opening and closing the window, and frame deterioration (rot/warping). All of these reduce energy efficiency and increase costs.

Your inspector will check each window but try to get a general idea of their age and condition before you make an offer. If the house needs all new windows, the cost will run into the thousands. This is a cost you need to consider when making an offer.

Plumbing

Your inspector will test the plumbing system, note any leaking faucets, showerheads, and toilets, and determine the water heater's age by checking the unit's label. If the water heater is operable but old and located in the attic, you should consider replacing it, as a leak could damage the interior of the house. If it is in the garage, all gas and some electric water heaters must be on a stand eighteen inches off the floor and should have an expansion tank. Straps are required in earthquake zones. Water heaters located inside the home should have a leak detection device to alert you if water begins to leak from the tank. It should also have a drain pan installed and a pipe that leads to the exterior of the home, in case the unit malfunctions.

Tankless water heaters are becoming more common due to their energy-saving features. They differ from tank water heaters: instead of heating and holding 40-50 gallons of water in a tank, they heat water only when you turn on the faucet, providing a continuous supply of hot water. Many buyers believe that "on demand" hot water is the same thing as "instant hot" hot water, and that the water will be hot as soon as you turn on the faucet. That is NOT the case. Although tankless water heaters instantly heat incoming water, they cannot make unheated water move any faster through the piping.

If you're buying an older home or one with large, mature trees, it's prudent to pay for a sewer line camera inspection to look for tree roots encroaching on underground pipes, cracks in pipes, or cast-iron pipes that are nearing the end of their life span.

Exposure

The direction a house faces is called its "exposure" and can affect the amount of natural light inside the home, heating and cooling costs, and maintenance. If the front of a house faces north, there is less natural light inside, but the backyard gets more sun in the summer. Homes facing south generally have more natural light indoors and backyard shade in the afternoon, which is desirable in warmer climates. Your lifestyle, the floor plan, and the location of the rooms will determine the home's comfort level.

Pests

Your lender (FHA/VA only) may require a certificate from your inspector stating that the home is free of termites and other critters. Even if it's not a lender requirement, you still need to know if the house has an active termite infestation or has been treated in the past. If prior treatments have been performed, determine whether they were partial treatments or if the entire house was treated. If only one side of the house is treated, termites will simply move from one side of the house to the other. A better strategy is to treat the entire house so that termites move to the neighbor's house rather than yours.

Also be mindful of squirrels, mice, rats, birds, and lizards that enter attics through small holes, gaps, or damaged areas, including vents, soffits, and rooflines. These critters have been known to cause significant damage by chewing electrical wires and causing fires, destroying insulation, damaging wood structures (rafters, beams, siding), ruining stored items, contaminating spaces with droppings, and creating entry points that lead to water leaks and mold.

Lead-Based Paint

Homes built before 1978 were usually painted with lead-based paint. The seller or their agent is required to give you the EPA booklet titled "Protect Your Family from Lead in Your Home" and must disclose any known lead-based paint hazards and send you any related documentation. The risk of lead-based paint exposure arises when children or pets ingest it, since lead can cause serious brain damage. Typically, homes originally painted with lead-based paint have been repainted multiple times over the years, substantially reducing the risk. As a rule, however, you are advised not to chew on the walls or windowsills!

Property Condition and Your Loan

Your lender may not approve your loan if the property's condition is un-acceptable to them. FHA and VA loans have minimum property standards that must be met for loan approval. Some of the issues that might cause a property to be rejected by your lender are:

1. Safety Issues

   - Mold or lead-based paint
   - Properties without heat
   - No sanitary sewage disposal
   - Termites or carpenter ants

2. Soundness

   - Damaged sheetrock
   - Extensive settlement (foundation issues)
   - Plumbing leaks
   - Roof near the end of its functional life

3. Security

   - Handrails, where appropriate
   - Frayed and damaged electrical wiring
   - Cracked or damaged exit doors

It's the job of the appraiser to alert the lender of any concerns about the condition of the property. Based on the appraiser's findings, the lender has the right to require an engineer's report or a repair to the property before they will approve your loan.

Don't make repairs and invest money into a home that you don't yet own! Lender-required repairs should be made by the seller, not by you. No exceptions!

Comparable Market Analysis (CMA)

A Comparable Market Analysis (CMA) is not the same as an appraisal. Real estate agents can create CMAs, but only a licensed appraiser can perform an appraisal. An appraiser's job is to determine a home's market value. They require specialized training and licensing that Realtors don't have. By contrast, a buyer's agents' job is to make sure your house will appraise for an amount equal to or greater than the sales price, and we do so by running a Comparable Market Analysis or CMA.

To create a CMA, your agent will use the MLS to research comparable properties in the area. After making rough adjustments for property condition, amenities, upgrades, and other factors, they will recommend a price *range* for the home. By reviewing the results, you will immediately learn whether the house is priced too high or too low. Homes in pristine condition should fall at the higher end of the range. Conversely, homes that need work fall in the lower end of the range.

It is very easy for agents to manipulate (deliberately or unknowingly) the numbers to make a home appear worth more or less than it is. If I want a home to appear like a good deal, I can select comps priced at the high end of the range, so the subject property looks cheap in comparison. I can also use comps to make an overpriced home appear at or below market value. An impartial appraisal conducted by a competent, well-trained appraiser prevents such market manipulation.

A far bigger issue than manipulated CMAs is the use of AI and automated valuations. Both are highly inaccurate but are seen by some Realtors and consumers as the holy grail of pricing models, when in fact they are the exact opposite. Zillow Zestimates, for example, uses public records data to guestimate a home's value. That might make logical sense when sale prices are public knowledge, but at least 12 states are "non-disclosure" states, meaning sale prices are shared only with Realtors and appraisers. In these cases, the Zestimate is based on an average price per square foot in the general area, or the home's tax-assessed value, which is usually substantially lower than the home's market value. In addition, the chosen comps are often not in the same neighborhood or comparable in size or condition.

Online valuations are a nonsensical way to determine a property's value.

Agents also use automated CMA software packages that make it easy to create beautiful CMA reports with minimal effort – but the results are mediocre at best. Most packages link to the MLS and auto-populate the home features used in the report. But if you've ever seen an MLS listing, you know the information provided is often insufficient, missing, or inaccurate, and, as the saying goes, "garbage in, garbage out." Some things – like accurately pricing a home – must be done manually.

Automation may benefit some aspects of real estate (like spamming people), but accurately pricing property is not one of them.

Ask your agent to send you all the raw data that they used in their report. Hopefully, they don't "accidentally on purpose" forget to send you a listing that could significantly impact the home's perceived value.

Price/Square Foot

Larger homes are priced lower per square foot, and smaller homes are priced higher per square foot. Why? The value of the land must be concentrated into the price of the home. The smaller the home, the more the value is concentrated.

For this reason (and others), it is *not* helpful to simply take the average price per square foot in the neighborhood and multiply it by the subject home's square footage to arrive at an offer. The listings need to be filtered before this calculation is performed. However, the unfiltered price per square foot *is* useful in tracking trends and ensuring that the home is priced comparably to other homes of the *same size and condition*. Just don't use this value to determine a home's market value or the amount you should pay for a home.

Seller's Disclosure Report

Sellers are required by law to disclose everything that they know about the property. From the seller's disclosure notice, you should be able to learn the age and condition of all the house's components. (Spoiler alert: you won't!)

Review this report carefully *before* submitting an offer and remember that the accuracy of these reports depends on the seller's knowledge of the property and their integrity.

> *It is not uncommon for sellers to stretch the truth or lie by omission to present their property in the most positive light. Always, always, always hire an inspector!*

In most cases, you have very little recourse if the seller fails to disclose the property's defects. Hiring an attorney can cost far more than the required repair, and I suspect most lawyers will tell you that it is extremely difficult to prove that the seller intended to commit fraud. Again, protect yourself by hiring a great inspector to evaluate the home's condition. Your inspector gets paid whether you buy the home or not, so they have no incentive to be dishonest.

Engineer Reports

If the seller's disclosure indicates that a repair has been made to the foundation, or if the seller has remodeled the property extensively, ask to see all the paperwork related to the repairs and improvements, and find out what kind of warranties exist, if any. *Ask specifically about existing engineer reports.* Proceed with caution whenever a structural defect is found and always hire your own structural engineer to evaluate the property's soundness.

Inspection Reports

Many homeowners keep the inspection report they received when purchasing the property. If they have one, they are required to share it with you. Although you can't negotiate repairs based on old reports, understanding the home's history is helpful and interesting. You may find items in the inspection report that the seller did not disclose. If nothing else, it's nice to have a record of the property's history.

Was the property under contract, and was it put back on the market shortly after? Find out why. If the terminating buyer performed an inspection and the seller or their agent has the report, the seller or their agent should share it. Do they? No, they don't, and practically speaking, there's not much you can do about it! It's very common for the listing agent and seller to refuse to receive the buyer's inspection report. If they don't look, they don't know. And if they don't know, they don't have to share. It's infuriating. I remain amazed and disappointed by the number of agents who cannot grasp the simple concept of full disclosure.

> *Operate under the assumption that sellers and listing agents are liars or omitters. Assume they are withholding relevant information and hire your own inspector to assess the home's condition.*

The standard seller's disclosure notice may not include all the components of a house; its contents vary by state. Don't be afraid to ask specific questions. How old is the HVAC? When was it last serviced? Can they explain the water stain on the living room ceiling? Did they refuse to receive or read an inspection report delivered to them by any other party?

Don't worry about looking like a jerk. Get the information that you need to feel comfortable moving forward with the transaction.

Tax Rolls

You or your agent can visit the county tax assessor's website to find a lot of information about the property. While you are investigating, try to uncover any of the following:

- Discrepancies in Square Footage - The square footage listed on the tax rolls can differ substantially from the square footage the seller claims on the MLS. A 100 square foot variance at $150 per square foot is $15,000! Know what you're buying. The MLS listing should list the seller's source when listing the square footage. The most accurate measurement would be one provided by an appraiser.

- Tax Assessed Value (TAV) - The TAV is *not* the same thing as market value; *do not assume for a second that the TAV is the price you should pay for the house*. You pay property taxes based on the TAV, which is typically lower than market value. If this figure is higher than what your agent told you the house was worth, investigate why this may be the case. Also, check whether the TAV has increased or decreased each year. If it is consistently trending downward, you may be in an area with depreciating values. Why are prices dropping? It could be that the area was overvalued in the first place, but you need to know for sure. Or it could simply reflect the overall real estate market.

- Ownership History Report - It's not hard to learn a property's ownership history. On the tax assessor's website, you should be able to learn when the seller purchased the house, from whom, and how many other previous owners there were. You can sometimes find out how much the seller paid and the amount of their original loan. It helps to know how much equity a homeowner has, if you can figure it out. If, for example, the seller owes more than what the house is worth at today's prices, the seller is "upside down" and will need to bring money to the closing table.

You need to make sure that they have the cash to sell the house. If not, you're dealing with a short sale transaction, which was discussed earlier.

Area Demographics

Most agents have access to demographic information and can present it to you in a very pretty package. The following types of information can be made available to you by your agent:

- Housing data, such as median estimated home value, median list price, median sales price, listing volume, sales volume, and sales counts
- People data, such as residents' average income and age, as well as their occupations, educational level, and voting trends
- Economic data, such as job growth and cost of living
- Quality of life data, such as climate and commute information

Don't rely on demographic reports to provide accurate pricing information. The only ways to value a home are with a Comparative Market Analysis or a formal appraisal.

Sales History

While the tax rolls can show you a history of previous owners of the home, your agent can give you an MLS report that displays the full history of a property, including the number of times a home was listed for sale or lease on the MLS, price drops, transactions that were cancelled, and more. You may get lucky and find old photos of the property to see what improvements have been made, if any. Use the information above, like pieces of a puzzle, to learn everything you can about the property and the seller before you write an offer and spend any money. Pay particular attention to the "days on market" for each listing. Is this a property that takes a very long time to sell? If so, find out why. Was it priced wrong, or is there something about the house that makes it unappealing to buyers? Find out, before the seller's problem becomes your problem.

Environmental Hazards

Sellers must disclose any known environmental hazards, including leaking underground oil tanks, asbestos, and lead pipes. Remedying these hazards can pose serious health risks and significant financial consequences. It is essential to understand what you are purchasing and the risks involved.

Floodplains

Your lender will require flood insurance if a home is in a floodplain. The extra expense may or may not be a deal-breaker, but you are entitled to know your risks and responsibilities before you sign. The seller must disclose this information to you, so look for it on the Seller's Disclosure notice. Better yet, play it safe and confirm whether the property is in a floodplain yourself by visiting http://www.floodsmart.gov/floodsmart/ to review the flood maps for your area. This is something your agent should be doing for you before you submit an offer.

Nuisance Factors

When touring a house, listen for things that may interfere with your enjoyment of the property, like barking dogs, traffic from local schools or restaurants, airplanes, trains, and noise from distant freeways. Remember, even if it doesn't bother you during the day, the noise may keep you up at night. Consider nuisance factors when evaluating a property's resale potential!

Most buyers are not interested in living in a home that backs up to a railroad track, freeway, or commercial property. Location, location, location!

CHAPTER FIVE

Offers and Negotiations

For some, negotiating the deal is the most stressful part of the home-buying process. How much should you offer? What if it's too high and you overpay? What if it's too low and you lose the house to another buyer? Are there competing offers? How low can you go without insulting the sellers and losing the deal?

Me? I love to negotiate the price and terms of a transaction. I love the strategizing, the opportunity to outsmart the competition, and the thrill of getting my clients a home they love at a great price. The sections that follow provide a detailed discussion of the negotiating process.

Structuring Your Offer – Laying the Groundwork

Before submitting an offer, your agent will call the seller's agent to discuss compensation. This call is the perfect time to gather information about why the sellers are moving, how anxious they are to sell, and potential competing offers. If the listing agent is begging for an offer, you can go in with a lower offer. If they have other offers, you'll need a different strategy.

Here are some good questions to ask before structuring your offer:

- Do they have any other offers?

- When does the seller prefer to close?
- Does the seller need a temporary lease-back?
- Have they already found a place to live?
- Is there any flexibility in the price?
- Is there a recent inspection report we can see?
- Is there anything else we should know about the property or seller?

Legally, the seller's agent isn't allowed to share information with you that might hurt their client's negotiating position, but you'd be surprised how forthcoming some inexperienced agents can be.

If the seller has a verbal agreement with a buyer and the parties are finalizing the paperwork, it's best to move on. You don't want to waste time and lose your second-choice home if your first choice is sold. But if you *really* love the house or haven't yet found a backup home, submit your offer anyway; the seller's agent is required to present it to the seller (unless the seller instructs the agent not to present any further offers). If your offer is strong enough, the seller may decide to work with you instead. The more likely scenario, however, is that they will use your offer to get more money or better terms from the first buyer. You won't know the outcome until you submit an offer. If nothing else, your contract can be in a backup position.

In highly competitive markets, when multiple offers are expected or received, the listing agent may request the highest and best offers and set a deadline. How do you know whether they really have multiple offers or are just trying to spark a bidding war? You don't. The seller's agent may state that they expect an offer on the property "any minute" and encourage you to submit an offer ASAP. They might tell you how many people have expressed interest in the house and try to convince you that the home will sell quickly. Or they could set an arbitrary deadline to submit an offer when they have no other offers on the table. These are obvious sales tactics used to generate an offer on the property. An experienced agent will pick up on inconsistencies and hints that the listing agent is bluffing. You won't ever know for sure if there are competing offers but remain mindful that the listing agent works for the seller, not for you. Just as I'm going to do everything in my power to secure the lowest price for my buyer/clients, the listing agent will do the opposite.

Think logically about the listing agent's responses. How long has the home been on the market? If it is a new listing and an exceptional house, the agent might be telling the truth, and it's safe to assume there will be multiple offers. If it has been on the market for a month or two without a recent price reduction, there probably is no bidding war, and the agent is playing games. This is where you need to rely on your agent's negotiating skills and integrity, and why it's so important to take your time and hire the right agent to represent you.

Points of Negotiation

Negotiating a house deal involves analyzing comparable sales ("comps"), understanding the seller's motivation, and leveraging inspection results to adjust the price or terms. This section discusses points of negotiation and how to get the best possible deal when negotiating the terms of a purchase money contract.

Price

Let's be honest – price trumps it all. Just as a buyer wants to pay as little as possible for a home, the seller wants to walk away with as much profit as they can. Buyers want to buy low; sellers want to sell high.

Most sellers are so hyper-focused on getting their price that they forget what matters most: their NET proceeds, or the amount of money they will put in their pocket after selling expenses are deducted. A good listing agent helps their clients evaluate an offer by providing a "net sheet" to clarify their bottom line. But buyers also need to understand the seller's net vs. gross proceeds and not focus solely on the sales price.

Some scenarios require you to make your best offer first; be careful about offering too much over the list price (unless the house is priced extremely low).

> *Your lender won't give you a blank check to buy anything you want! The house needs to appraise for at least the sales price.*

If it doesn't appraise, you are required to make up the difference by restructuring your loan, putting down more cash, or negotiating a new sales price with the seller.

Before submitting a crazy, high offer, consider the consequences. If you negotiated a sales price of $350,000, would you still want to own it if the appraiser valued it at $300,000? Do you have the cash to do so? If the answer is yes, ask yourself how long you plan to live in the home. It will take time to recoup the $50,000 you overpaid for the house. What would you do if you lost your job and needed to sell? Or get transferred? Know the answer to these questions before you put your financial future at risk.

Submitting a crazy, low-ball offer has consequences as well. First, sellers have financial and emotional investments in their property, and low-ball offers make them feel disrespected and could cause them to shut down negotiations before they start. The buyer is viewed as a time waster and someone who isn't serious about the property; all parties (including your own agent) will start to ignore you. If the seller does make a counteroffer, they are more likely to be less flexible and more hostile during the negotiating process. If you're going to submit a low-ball offer, it should be supported by market data, not just a "throw spaghetti against the wall and see what sticks" mentality.

Option Fee & Earnest Money

The option fee (the terminology varies by state, but the concept remains the same) is the money a buyer pays to a seller to have the option to terminate the sales contract within a specific period, often 5-10 days. The option period (also negotiable) gives the buyer time to inspect the house, negotiate repairs, and terminate the contract for *any* reason, while prohibiting the seller from selling the house to another buyer. The only penalty the buyer faces for terminating is the loss of their option fee.

Sellers prefer a large option fee since more money reduces the likelihood that the buyer will terminate the contract. A small amount of option money makes it very easy for the buyer to tie up the house for the duration of the option period and walk away with little penalty or loss. Do you want to make the seller comfortable enough to take their house off the market for you? Offer a decent amount of option money and a shorter option period.

Option fee funds should not be confused with earnest money. Earnest money is a security deposit that demonstrates the buyer's commitment to purchasing the property and shows good or "earnest" faith. Generally, you want to keep the earnest money to a minimum to protect your interests, but high enough that the seller takes your offer seriously. If you're buying in a hot market, offering a higher earnest money deposit is a wise move. In a sluggish market, you can get away with less. The amount is negotiable, but a commonly used figure is 1%-3% of the sales price. Earnest money is placed in a trust account, usually at the title or settlement company, and is refundable under most (but not all) conditions:

- Canceling a contract during your option or due diligence period? Refundable.
- Canceling due to a low appraisal? Refundable if an appraisal contingency is in place.
- Canceling because your loan was denied? Refundable when termination takes place according to the terms of your financing contingency.
- Did you freak out, change your mind, or cancel a week before you're scheduled to close? Non-refundable. And a good way to get yourself sued.

Contract contingencies are built into sales contracts to protect both the buyer and the seller and are discussed again in greater detail later in the chapter.

Some states refer to the "option period" as the "due diligence period." Some states require the buyer to pay the seller to remove the home from the market, while others allow the buyer a due diligence period at no additional cost. Your agent can explain the standard procedures in your state.

Closing Date

Selling a home can be as stressful as buying one. The seller might be under contract to purchase a different home, but they often can't qualify for their new mortgage until their current home has sold and closed. Or they prefer not to vacate their property until after closing, so they don't have to pay two housing payments. All their plans are contingent upon the buyer. Anything a buyer can do to make it easier on the seller will often mean more to the seller than cash.

Accommodating the seller's preferred closing date is an easy way to steal a house from another buyer.

If a house is vacant, the seller will be happy with a quick closing. In my area, a fast closing is three weeks. If you can close quickly, the seller may accept a lower price, since they won't have to pay next month's mortgage on an empty home. If the house is still occupied, however, the seller may have nowhere to go. In this case, offering them a temporary lease could win you the deal. Working around their schedule and making their move as easy as possible can save you thousands or help you win the house in a competitive market.

Possession

A seller vacating and a buyer taking possession of a property can create many potential conflicts. Sellers do not want to leave their homes until they are sure that the transaction will close, and buyers are not always comfortable with sellers living in homes they have just purchased. What if they won't leave?

In some states, sellers are given 48 hours to vacate the property after closing. The buyers can take possession right after funding if the property is vacant. In other states, the sellers vacate the property before closing.

The terms of possession are negotiable and must be agreed upon before you execute your purchase offer, and the specifics *must* be committed to in writing!

> *You should never, ever, ever let the sellers stay in the home after closing without a signed Temporary Lease Agreement. Ever.*

If the sellers refuse to vacate the property, you will need a lease to evict them. Removing squatters from your property - particularly without a signed lease - is long, complicated, and expensive.

If the seller will only be leasing the property for 48 hours, I generally don't request a deposit or rent (exceptions apply); I consider it a goodwill gesture. If my buyer makes it easy for them to move, I hope they will reciprocate by taking good care of the property and cleaning the house on their way out. If the seller plans to stay any longer than that, I will retain a security deposit from the seller's proceeds if the property is damaged. If they leave without incident, the money is promptly returned. Be sure to include a holdover fee in your lease, so if the seller doesn't move out on time, you will be compensated; make it steep.

Closing Costs

When a seller pays your closing costs, you benefit because it takes less cash to buy the house. Technically, you're not saving the money; the closing costs get rolled into the sales price or into your mortgage. However, it makes it easier for qualified buyers who are short on cash to purchase a home.

Sellers won't have a problem paying your closing costs because they are only concerned about their net, or the amount of money that goes into their pocket after closing. An offer of $205,000 with a $5,000 seller contribution toward the buyer's closing costs nets $200,000 for the seller. It's the equivalent of receiving an offer for $200,000 with no seller contribution. To the seller, these two offers are the same. For the buyer, however, the $5,000 is important because it reduces the amount of money they bring to the closing table. In some cases, that's the difference between being able to buy a house or not.

Note that most lenders limit the seller's contribution to 3-6% of the sales price, and contributions can't be used toward your down payment. Check with your lender regarding any limits or restrictions specific to your chosen financing, and keep in mind that financing is subject to an appraisal. You can't roll unlimited amounts into the sales price without valuation issues.

Negotiating Strategies

After your offer is presented to the seller, they can accept it, reject it, or make a counteroffer. Remember that everything is negotiable, not just the price. Over the past thirty years in the industry, I have observed several patterns in how sellers respond to the offers I submit on behalf of my clients. They include the following.

The Cave

The seller accepts the offer as-is. They agree to the price, closing date, home warranty, title policy, and closing costs, among other terms. This scenario happens with a desperate or anxious seller, or with offers so strong that the seller can't refuse. They won't risk losing a strong buyer by making a counteroffer. This doesn't happen often, which is probably a good thing; when it does, buyers worry they've left money on the table or that something is wrong with the house. Why is the seller so anxious to execute a contract? It may have nothing to do with the house. They may have been transferred or recently divorced and must move quickly. They might have lost their job and need to tap into their equity to make ends meet. You may never know.

Don't second-guess your offers and talk yourself out of a great deal when you have limited information about the seller and their situation.

Seller Counters $1000 Below List Price

Suppose a home is listed for $400,000, and you submit an offer for $350,000. The seller is unhappy with your offer and is countering at $399,000. This tactic generally indicates they believe your initial offer is too low, but they want to work with you because they consider you a strong buyer. *This is an invitation to submit a better offer.*

This tactic rarely results in a deal. The sellers are insulted and angry at the buyers' offer, and the buyers are angry at the sellers' response.

This response from the seller provides a lot of information about their circumstances and motivation: they are not desperate and will not give the house away. Try again, but next time, don't waste their time.

Don't be upset if a seller counters this way! If the house was good enough to make an offer on in the first place, it's good enough for you to swallow your pride and submit a new offer. You took a swing, and you missed. Take another swing.

Baby Steps

Here, the seller responds to your offer by dropping the price by $3,000-$4,000, for example. As a serious buyer, you respond by coming up by $3,000-$4000, and so forth. The parties go back and forth until one party claims it is their final offer, usually after the third round. This strategy usually results in a pleasant transaction, with both parties giving and taking, and considering the other party's needs.

Split the Difference

Some sellers hate negotiating and view it as confrontational; some agents hate it too. These types just want to split the difference and get it over with. I've found that it is usually quite easy to get the seller to reduce their asking price further in this scenario, if not with the price, then on other negotiable items like repairs. This is a seller who can be negotiated with, within reason.

Reject or No Response

When buyers make ridiculous offers, it's not uncommon for the seller to reject them without a counteroffer. They may send an invitation to submit a new offer, but they won't bother negotiating.

A lot of buyers get upset when they don't get a response, and they shouldn't; ridiculous offers don't warrant a response. Real estate is a game made for serious players.

I don't mind submitting low offers when a house is overpriced, needs a lot of work, or when I can defend my buyer's position. However, touring a house, researching a property, and submitting an offer takes at least 3 to 4 hours of my time, and I don't get paid for my efforts. I don't want to spend my time writing low-ball offers that have no chance of getting accepted, any more than the seller's agent wants to present them to her client.

What Not to Do

Some buyers are their own worst enemies during the negotiating process. Here are some things buyers do during negotiations that cost them money or the house.

Complain About the House

Some inexperienced buyers like to present the seller with a long list of perceived problems with the house to justify a low offer. This "I'm doing you a favor by buying your home" attitude does nothing but antagonize the seller and creates a hostile, risky transaction. If the buyer is making an offer to purchase a property, they clearly like the house and see value in owning it. If the seller has an opportunity to sell the home to someone more pleasant, they will. Or they won't take care of the property and will leave it in poor condition once they move. Play nice or pay a price.

Use Their Heart, Not Their Head

The homebuying process is tedious, stressful, and, at times, exhausting. There are few decisions greater than this one! By the time you pick a house, you will be emotionally invested. This is where you really need a good agent to be your voice of reason. Control your emotions until after repairs have been negotiated and you are sure it is a good house.

Overpay Out of Fear

There are times when you must submit your best offer first, but often there is plenty of room for negotiation. Take an objective look at the seller's situation, the general real estate climate in your area, and the raw data that your agent provides to see how long it takes similar homes to sell. If the home has a unique feature that can't be found anywhere else, you may need to pay more. If you can find a home like this one on any given block, don't submit your best offer right away.

Waive Contingencies

A contingency in your contract will allow you to back out of the deal without penalty if certain things go wrong. Sellers usually don't want to agree to these clauses because they risk tying up their property for several weeks or more only to have the buyer walk away before closing. That's fair. However, buyers assume the risk when purchasing a home and have the right to know what they are buying, its value, and their responsibilities once they close on the house. Sellers and their agents can't be trusted to provide this information accurately; buyers (with their agent's help) must uncover and verify certain details themselves. Contingencies protect buyers from the unknown. That's fair too.

In hot markets, buyers often naively agree to waive some or all their contingencies. The following pages discuss the contract contingencies written into most contracts, and the risk of waiving them.

Financing Contingency

A financing contingency states that your offer is contingent on securing financing for the property within a specified period. It specifies the type of financing, the terms, and the timeframe for obtaining loan approval. Unless you are buying a home with cash, are fully approved, or are extremely confident in your loan approval, you should always include a financing contingency. If your financing falls through, your earnest money deposit will be refunded.

Fifteen to twenty days is usually plenty of time for you to secure financing. The deal does not have to close in this timeframe, but you should have your loan approved with "conditions." Conditional loan approval means that the bank will lend you money once certain conditions are met, like the appraisal, job verification, a certain bank statement, a survey, and so forth. But your file has been approved through automated underwriting, processed, and submitted to the underwriter for conditional loan approval. It's far along in the process.

<u>Risks of Waiving Your Financing Contingency</u>

- You could lose your earnest and option money
- The money you spent on inspections and appraisals will be lost
- The seller can sue you for breach of contract
- If you have significant assets like a retirement account, you could be forced to buy the house without financing

If you decide it's necessary to waive your financing contingency to be competitive in an aggressive seller's market, talk to your lender about submitting your file for full underwriting approval before you do. Let them know you intend to waive your financing contingency so they can make you aware of any potential deficiencies with your loan file.

Appraisal Contingency

The appraisal contingency has become increasingly important in some parts of the country, where a competitive market is driving prices higher. This contingency says that if the house does not appraise for at least the purchase price, you can back out of the deal without penalty. Waiving your financing contingency means that you agree to buy the house at the agreed upon price, regardless of the appraised value. So, if the sales price is $400,000 but the house appraises for $350,000, you must still buy the house, even if it means coming up with an additional $50,000 or restructuring your loan. Waiving the appraisal contingency strengthens your offer, as it gives the seller assurance that the buyer can't terminate the transaction due to a low appraisal and won't be asked to reduce their price midway through.

Risks of Waiving Your Appraisal Contingency

If the house does not appraise for the sales price, the bank will not lend you the money you need to buy the house; you will be forced to cover the difference between the sales price and the appraised value either in cash or through restructuring your loan. Instead of putting 20% down, for example, you could put 5% down and use the other 15% to cover the shortage in cash. If restructuring your loan or bringing extra money to closing isn't an option, you can't buy the house. Your loan will be denied.

The risks associated with waiving your appraisal contingency can be severe. How do you feel about paying above market value for a home? Do you plan to own the home long enough to recoup the money you spent to purchase this property? If you are forced to use your down payment funds to make up the shortage in value (for example, putting 5% down instead of 20% down), are you comfortable with the higher mortgage payment, which will now include mortgage insurance? Will you qualify for your mortgage with the lower down payment, higher DTI, and less cash reserves? You MUST understand the consequences of waiving this contingency before you agree to do it.

I never recommend that a buyer sign a full appraisal waiver, although I've had several do it. (Cringe).

Instead of a full appraisal waiver, submit a partial waiver.

A partial waiver means you can put a "floor" at which you can terminate the contract. Let's assume you're purchasing a house for $400,000 and are comfortable spending $25,000 above the appraised value. You can include a partial waiver with a floor of $375,000. That is, if the appraisal comes in *below* $375,000, you can terminate the contract and have your earnest money refunded. But if the appraisal comes in above $375,000, you would be required to pay the difference in cash at closing. In this case, the partial waiver limits the amount you'll pay above the appraised value to $25,000. This strategy is not as appealing to a seller compared to a full waiver, but you'll still be more competitive compared to not signing a waiver at all.

Inspection Contingency

Offers that waive a home inspection contingency are more attractive to home sellers because the buyers are purchasing the property as-is/where-is. The sellers won't be required to make repairs or to reduce their price to compensate the buyer for an unknown or undisclosed issue with the property.

Risks of Waiving Your Home Inspection

A home inspection is something that protects your financial interest in what will likely be the largest purchase you make in your life, one in which you need as much information as possible. For example, learning that a home needs repairs costing $20,000 or more could change your decision to buy it or the amount you're willing to spend. If you're buying a relatively new home, waiving your inspection period isn't nearly as problematic. But waiving your inspection on homes, even a few years old, can be a risky proposition. If you won't have the funds to make unexpected repairs after closing, don't even consider waiving your inspection.

Another option: Buy the house as-is, but don't waive the right to back out of the contract if something major is wrong.

Most small repairs, like minor plumbing leaks, dirty a/c coils, and an old water heater, won't break the bank for most buyers. But repairing a bad roof, electrical system, or foundation is not a cost you want to incur after closing.

Waiving repairs but not your right to terminate the contract if a major defect is a far smarter and safer strategy than waiving your inspection completely.

HOA Contingency

An HOA (Homeowner's Association) contingency allows a homebuyer to review HOA documents (bylaws, financials, rules) and cancel the purchase if they find the rules too restrictive or the financials problematic, such as insufficient reserve funds or unexpected special assessments. Your earnest money is refunded upon termination.

Since it can take several weeks to receive these documents from the HOA, the buyer often has the right to cancel the contract a week or two before closing. Sellers, understandably, prefer buyers who are willing to waive the HOA contingency.

Risks of Waiving the HOA Contingency

Regardless of how strict or permissive an HOA's bylaws might be, all buyers should be aware of ongoing litigation, homeowner and HOA disputes, and any special assessments. If you're buying a property as an investment or plan to convert the home to a rental property in the future, it's imperative that you confirm the HOA's policies on rental property in the area. The same is true if you plan to own livestock or place an ADU (Accessory Dwelling Unit) on the property. The decision to waive the HOA contingency should not be taken lightly.

Before waiving this contingency, visit the HOA's website. Many of them now post their documents online. Feel free to contact the HOA directly to ask questions or to request copies of any documents you'd like to review prior to submitting an offer.

Counteroffers & Acceptance

Once you make your initial offer, the seller will respond using one of the strategies mentioned above. Rely on your agent to assist you with formulating a negotiating plan that will help you accomplish your goal.

I recommend you keep asking for discounts until the seller says "no" twice. If, for example, you have gone several rounds with the seller and they come back with their best and final offer, don't believe them. Make another counteroffer and see what happens. It doesn't always have to be about price; ask for another concession, such as a repair or a closing-cost concession. Accept the offer if they refuse and stand by what they claimed is their bottom line. Remember, the seller needs to net a certain amount from the sale to pay off their mortgage, cover closing costs, and buy their next home. Just like you have a top, they have a bottom. During negotiations, your aim is to keep shooting arrows until you find what appears to be their bottom.

Try to remain logical and keep your emotions out of the bargaining process. Feeling anxious, excited, desperate, or angry can impact the outcome of negotiations.

Buying in a Seller's Market

A seller's market is one in which there are more buyers than sellers; buyers must compete for the relatively few homes for sale. Competing offers drive up prices, and buyers must spend more to get what they want.

Buying a home in a seller's market can be a frustrating experience. With some sellers receiving 5-30 offers within a day of listing their home, it's important to draft a contract that appeals to the seller but also makes sense for you. It's not uncommon for a buyer to become so anxious to win a bid that they throw common sense out the window. Don't get so caught up in the game that you make poor decisions that can potentially cost you tens of thousands of dollars! It's better to stay in an apartment for a few extra months than it is to overpay for a home or to assume a lot of financial risk. Determine your budget and your bottom line, and don't budge!

Negotiating in a Seller's Market

The perfect contract – from a seller's perspective – would be all cash. The seller wouldn't have to pay for a title policy, closing costs, or repairs, and the buyer would waive all contingencies. The buyer's perspective is the exact opposite, of course. When writing an offer in a seller's market, consider the following:

Down Payment/Loan Terms

If a cash buyer is the ideal buyer, the next best option is a buyer with a large down payment (20% or more). Why? Simply put, a buyer who puts more money down has a better chance of closing the deal. Low down payment loans are more likely to be declined, and they weaken a buyer's position in a seller's market. In addition, buyers who are strapped for cash probably won't have cash to close the deal if the house doesn't appraise and the seller is unwilling to drop their price. Does that mean you can't compete if you don't have a lot of money to put down? Of course, not. Just know that this is an area where your contract will be weak. Try to make up for it elsewhere.

Seller Paid Closing Costs

Sellers typically care only about how much money they keep after a transaction closes. Rather than offering a higher sales price that might cause a problem with the appraisal, you can offer to pay some of the fees that sellers customarily pay at closing. The title policy, home warranty, real estate commissions, legal fees, and transfer fees are common closing costs typically paid by the seller. You can increase the seller's net proceeds by paying some of these costs without having an adverse effect on your appraisal.

Close Quickly but Lease Back

Make it as easy as possible for the seller to move. Close quickly so the seller's funds are available to purchase their new home but give them time to vacate the property so they can move directly into their new home without needing temporary housing. If the property is vacant, a quick closing means the seller doesn't have to make another mortgage payment. Consider the seller's needs and accommodate them when you can.

Buying in a Buyer's Market

A buyer's market is one in which there are more sellers than buyers; sellers must compete for the relatively small number of buyers seeking a home. The lack of competition causes prices to drop, allowing buyers to purchase a property at a far lower price than they would in a balanced or seller's market.

It's far more fun to buy a home in a buyer's market than a seller's market. Listing agents and sellers are practically begging for offers. In fact, many sellers will throw in the cat and their firstborn child for free! They will replace the carpet, wash your car, make you dinner – name it. I can confirm...it's pretty great.

Negotiating in a Buyer's Market

Writing an offer in a buyer's market means your initial offer can be less aggressive. Option fees can be lower, and option periods can be longer. You can extend closing, put up less earnest money, and the seller will be far more willing to pay for the title policy, warranty, and other expenses. Except for touring dozens of homes, buying a home in a buyer's market is glorious! *Until it isn't.*

Seller's markets are growth markets. Prices are rising, properties are selling, and the economy is strong. Sellers want to time the market and sell at the peak. Even if they miss (as they usually do), they still make money.

By contrast, a buyer's market means the market is declining. Prices are dropping, and you want to buy at the bottom of the market. But, since it's impossible to time the market, you could negotiate what you think is a great deal and still see your home's value drop, at least in the short term. There's nothing fun about losing money, regardless of the circumstances.

If you miss the bottom of a buyer's market, don't worry. Eventually, a declining market becomes a growth market. Buyer's markets become seller's markets. Buy a quality house with a good floor plan, in a good location. Eventually, you'll get your money out and hopefully make a nice profit.

"Love Letters" to the Seller

Homebuyers trying to stand out from a crowd of contracts are sometimes advised to include a personal letter with their offer. Appealing to the seller as a person, rather than as a contract, can sometimes give a buyer an emotional edge. I've seen them work more than a few times.

Be aware that love letters can subject the buyer, seller, and brokers to potential violations of the Fair Housing Laws of the Federal, State, and local governments because they often innocently mention or distinguish classes of protected persons, for example:

- "I can see our family waking up on Christmas morning here;"
- "Our son is the star of his basketball team;"
- "We want to send our children to the parochial school and church in the neighborhood;"
- "The house has a great dining room just right for our large Italian family dinners."

The above statements reveal the buyer's ethnicity, family status, marital status, and other personal information. If such a letter contributes to the seller's acceptance or denial of the purchase offer, it may violate Fair Housing Law.

Because of the risk of violations, some listing agents (the smart ones) refuse to receive or read love letters, and they advise their seller clients to do the same.

Your agent should be able to craft a well-written cover letter to plead your case in a way that does not violate fair housing regulations, eliminating the need for a love letter. If my buyers insist on including a love letter, I am required to include it with our offer, but I warn them that the letter may not be presented to the seller.

If you insist on sending a love letter, follow the tips below:

- Flatter the Seller. Tell the seller how great their taste is and how much you love their impressive collection of ceramic cats over the fireplace. Lay it on thick but keep it sincere.
- Be direct. The more streamlined your message is, the more memorable it will be. If it's a hot property, the seller might be reviewing fifteen other offers and love letters. Yours needs to stand out.
- Paint a picture. Tell the seller, "I'd be so happy in the summer to entertain friends in your outdoor kitchen." Doing so will create a visual memory for them and may help you get noticed.
- Don't redecorate their house. Are you planning on changing the landscaping? Keep it quiet. They may have buried their dog under the tree you're planning to pave over. Even if the seller has horrible taste, most are still emotionally attached and protective of their homes.
- Sell Your Sanity. Present yourself as a stable buyer who can close the deal. Whether it is a reference to your lack of contingencies, excellent credit, or stellar employment record, it eases the sellers' fears that the transaction will fall apart at the last minute.
- Be humble. Show humility and ask the seller to accept your offer. "We'd be honored to live in your home," or "I hope our offer is what you're looking for," goes a long way in generating goodwill and appreciation for their time. The ball is in the seller's court, and your letter should acknowledge that.

- Don't whine. The seller doesn't care that your rent just increased or that you've lost out on five other homes. Keep your letter upbeat and enthusiastic. Sellers want to sell to a winner, not a whiner.
- Close with appreciation. Thank the seller for taking the time to read the ode you wrote about your unworthy self. "Thank you so much for your time," or even "We're honored to have the opportunity," will leave the seller with the understanding that you value their consideration (although your agent will probably respect you a lot less).

Inspections & Negotiating Repairs

You *must* hire a professional inspector to inspect every square inch of the house and report their findings, even if the seller has a recent inspection report. Your inspector should be licensed, experienced, and recommended by a friend, co-worker, or agent. Be aware, however, of potential conflicts of interest if you rely on a recommendation from your Realtor. Some agents recommend inspectors because they won't kill the deal by scaring the buyer. Or they recommend the inspector they find to be the friendliest and most charismatic, regardless of their qualifications or skills. Or the ones that send cookies and gift cards over the holidays.

I recommend inspectors based on the quality of their reports, but I don't have personal relationships with them, nor have I met most of them. I usually don't attend inspections so my clients can discuss the house's condition with a neutral party to the transaction. The inspector gets paid whether the deal closes or not! The same cannot be said for real estate agents. If I have a question about an item on the report, I email the inspector and always include my client in the communication. Inspectors work for my clients, not for me, and I welcome their advice and expertise.

A good inspection should take about three to four hours, depending on the size of the house. In the end, you will have a list of items that need repair or replacement and will have learned how to maintain the property. Your inspector should go through each item with you. Be sure you understand the report so you can make informed decisions when requesting repairs from the seller.

Negotiating Repairs

Even when buying new construction, you don't get a perfect house. Don't expect the seller to agree to all the repairs, and don't confuse a repair with an improvement.

Repairs are made to things that are broken. An air conditioner that isn't cooling, a leaking faucet, or a broken doorbell are examples of items that need repair. Replacing carpet, installing granite, or painting the exterior are *improvements*, not repairs. Most sellers will consider making repairs but will reject improvements, and rightfully so. When negotiating repairs, consider the following.

Roof

Your inspector will assess the roof's condition and estimate its remaining life. If there is existing damage from hail, wind, or another insured event, be sure that the seller files a claim with their insurance company, and *do not* close until the roof is either replaced or the money is held in escrow (the title company keeps the money and pays the roofer once the repair has been made). This is non-negotiable, as you may have difficulty obtaining homeowners' insurance for the property if there is existing damage. And if the property is not insurable, your loan will be denied.

> *Do not incur any additional expenses until this issue is resolved! If you must walk away from the house, you want to minimize your losses.*

Sprinkler system

Apart from broken sprinkler heads, I don't like my clients to assume the risk of a broken sprinkler system. Repairs can be expensive, and leaks are hard to locate. Have the seller make any repairs before closing.

Appliances

Only built-in appliances are usually included in the sale of a home (this varies by state). Ovens, ranges, built-in microwaves, and dishwashers are consumables and relatively low-cost items to repair/replace. If these items are working when you close on the house, they should be covered by any home warranty that you hopefully have in place.

Foundation

I can live with a few piers installed as a preventive measure, and I don't automatically walk away from a house with a foundation issue in a neighborhood known to have a high percentage of failing foundations. I can also live with a historic home whose pier-and-beam foundation requires reinforcement. But often, I advise my clients to walk away from a home with structural defects.

> *One of the riskiest things you can do is to buy a home that needs, or has had, a foundation repair or structural damage.*

Not only can the house be damaged during the repair (particularly the plumbing), but you also can't be sure that the repair will hold. In addition, when it's time to sell, you must – by law – disclose the repair to potential homebuyers. Many won't want to assume the risk, and you'll have no choice but to sell the property below market value. While it's true that some foundation repair companies offer lifetime transferable warranties on their work, you can't trust the foundation repair company to honor your claim or to be in business for as long as you own the house. Leave foundation issues to the investors and the buyers who have bad karma coming their way.

> *If you are considering buying a home with a foundation issue, ALWAYS hire a structural engineer during your inspection so you understand your risks. Don't expect a foundation repair company to accurately assess the property. They offer free foundation inspections to sell you a foundation repair. Spend a few hundred dollars on a structural engineer.*

Air Conditioners and Heaters

Both air conditioning and heating units can be extremely costly to repair or replace, and you should insist that the seller make any necessary repairs before closing. It is crucial to clean the A/C coils if they are dirty; this often happens when homeowners fail to change the filters regularly. Because this is a maintenance item, cleaning the coils is typically excluded from your home warranty and is an expense you shouldn't incur. The HVAC should have been serviced recently and be in warrantable condition before you close.

Windows

One of the most common issues I see pertains to double-pane windows. When air gets between the two panes of glass in a double-pane window, it can lead to condensation and fog. The only fix is to replace the glass. I typically advise my clients to request replacement of foggy windows in highly visible locations. If most of the windows are faulty, I recommend replacing all the windows or accepting cash in lieu, as the total cost to replace them will be thousands of dollars.

Cosmetic improvements

Paint, new fixtures, flooring, caulking, and sealant are cosmetic improvements, not repairs. I always recommend that my clients address these items after settlement. It's not uncommon for sellers to try to save money by making repairs themselves, but the results aren't always good. If the home needs substantial cosmetic updates, hopefully you have negotiated a lower sales price when you submitted an offer to compensate you for your time and expense.

Plumbing & Electrical

Except for minor items, the seller needs to make most plumbing and electrical repairs (but not improvements). It's perfectly reasonable to expect the seller to fix leaking faucets, outlets that don't work, and to make repairs to the hot water heater (particularly if it's in the attic, since a leaking water heater can cause significant damage to the home). It's not reasonable, in most cases, to ask the seller to bring a house built to code in 1988 to current standards.

Repair Allowances

Under certain circumstances, you may wish to ask for cash in lieu of repairs or in addition to certain repairs. As previously mentioned, certain repairs are best handled by the buyer after closing. Often, sellers prefer not to deal with the inconvenience of repairing the property; psychologically, they have already moved on to the next house. Talk to your agent about the cost to repair specific items, then see what the sellers are willing to do.

When to Walk Away

It's perfectly reasonable to expect to buy a home with a solid roof and working electrical, plumbing, heating, and cooling systems. If these items are functioning but nearing the end of their lifespan, you should buy the home below market value (i.e., at the low end of the range on your CMA). If they are non-functional, negotiate the repair or a repair allowance. Most problems can be fixed. The only question is this: who pays for it?

But what about the more significant issues? How do you know when to walk away, and what is considered significant? Issues such as severe foundation problems, toxic mold, collapsing sewer lines beneath the house, multiple termite treatments, a basement that floods frequently, asbestos, and radon are all good reasons to pass on a home. If you're working with a good agent, they can usually (but not always) help you steer clear of the obvious "dogs" before you spend money on option fees, inspections, and appraisals. But surprises happen, and it's often nobody's fault. The seller may not be aware that tree roots have penetrated the water lines under the house, and the presence of radon gas is not obvious to the world.

If a problem is uncovered during your due diligence period, rely on professional opinions to help you decide your next move. If a structural engineer has concerns, you should, too. Talk to a few plumbers and get quotes. See what the seller is willing to do to address these issues. But never, ever, ever buy someone else's problems unless you are buying the property cheap enough to justify both the expense of making repairs and the risk of future unknowns.

Deaths in a Home

Most (but not all) states require that violent deaths be disclosed; this is not true for natural deaths. Some have specific time frames for disclosing murders and suicides, say three years. Other states don't require voluntary disclosure at all but do require the seller to tell the truth if asked by the buyer about deaths in the home. Violent deaths like murders or suicides are considered "stigmatizing events" and can affect property values. Natural deaths or accidents don't have the same impact on property values but still upset some buyers. If you are a buyer sensitive to this issue, be sure to ask the seller about the property's history. You can also Google the property address to see if any news stories can be found about the house and neighborhood.

> *Air conditioners and roofs can be replaced. But the stench of a double homicide in the house lives forever.*

CHAPTER SIX

All About Mortgages

I started talking about predatory lending and improper homebuying practices over 30 years ago. I received a lot of hate mail and even a few anony-
mous death threats from mortgage 'professionals' who did not like what I was
saying about the industry. Yes, death threats!

Today, lenders are required to be far more transparent in their pricing and
loan programs. There are more regulations, including the requirement that
mortgage loan officers be licensed, pass background checks, and maintain
high educational standards.

I spend a lot of time educating my clients before we ever really talk seriously about buying. The following pages are intended to "give it to you in a
nutshell." Education is vital if we are to continue eliminating predatory lending practices. Let's get started.

Some Definitions

It's not necessary to deep dive into the world of mortgages to shop for a
mortgage and a good lender, but it IS necessary to understand some basic

terms and concepts. The list below is the terminology you need to understand.

Closing costs

Closing costs are *all* the fees and expenses paid to finalize a loan, including application fees, origination fees, credit reports, appraisals, processing, title insurance, homeowners' insurance, underwriting, and document preparation. Some closing costs are collected upfront (such as appraisal and credit report fees), while others (such as processing fees and title policies) are collected at closing.

Origination fees

Origination fees are one-time, upfront charges paid to the lender to cover the cost of financing your home; they are usually a percentage of the loan amount. This fee may be collected to pay loan officers, processors, admin fees, or any other legitimate charge associated with originating your loan. Origination fees can be paid in cash at closing, added to the loan amount, paid through a lender's credit, or paid from a seller's contribution toward the buyer's closing costs or pre-paids.

Discount Points

Discount points are prepaid interest. They are expressed as a percentage of the loan amount and are charged only when the buyer wants an interest rate below market rates. One point is equal to one percent of the loan amount, three points are equal to three percent of the loan amount, and so forth. Example: If you are quoted an interest rate of 7.25% with zero points, but you have your heart set on 7%, you could pay one point to lower the rate to that level.

One point, or 1% of the loan amount, generally translates to a 0.25% reduction in the interest rate, although it can vary by lender and market conditions.

Yield Spread Premiums (YSP)

Yield Spread Premiums are commissions paid by wholesale lenders to retail lenders or brokers for writing loans that are above "par" or market interest rates. If, for example, you qualify for an interest rate of 8%, but your loan officer can get you to pay 8.5%, the wholesale lender will pay your broker an extra commission called a Yield Spread Premium.

YSPs are also used to keep the borrower's out of pocket costs to a minimum. The broker charges a higher rate to earn more commission and then pays some of the buyer's closing costs. If you see a lender offering a "no closing cost" loan, the lender is being paid through a YSP rather than an upfront origination fee.

Until recently, banks had an advantage over brokers because they were not required to disclose their commissions to borrowers/clients. Brokers, however, *were* required to make the disclosure, and borrowers who understood YSPs didn't like what they learned! Recent regulations have leveled the playing field for mortgage brokers, and *they are no longer required to disclose their YSP to clients.*

If a loan officer tells you that Yield Spread Premiums don't exist, they are either uninformed or dishonest. The YSP hasn't gone away; only the requirement to make the disclosure has.

Prepayment Penalties

A prepayment penalty is a fee a lender charges when you pay off all or a large portion of your loan early; it compensates the lender for the interest they would have earned over the loan's full term. Most modern mortgages don't have a pre-payment penalty, but if paying off your mortgage quickly (within 1 to 5 years) is something you plan to do, make sure you don't have a prepayment penalty on your loan and that you won't be penalized when you do so.

Rate Lock

Mortgage rates can change daily and sometimes hourly. Locking your interest rate means your rate won't change between the time you lock the rate and the time you close, provided there are no significant changes to your loan application (such as a drop in income, credit, or verifiable income). Locks protect you from paying a higher rate when rates are rising but can hurt you if rates are falling since you can't lower your rate once it's locked. Most lenders offer a free 30-day lock. If your transaction doesn't close within 30 days, you'll have to pay for a lock extension or pay the current market interest rate.

If you are comfortable floating your interest rate for a couple of weeks, you can usually get a better price on loans with a 15-day lock. Ask your loan officer to show you the difference between a 30-day and a 15-day lock but remember that interest rates are just as likely to rise as to drop. Until you lock, you're taking a risk.

PITI

PITI is an acronym that stands for Principal, Interest, Taxes, and Insurance. The *principal* is the amount of the payment applied to your loan balance. *Interest* is the cost of borrowing the money to buy the house. *Taxes* refer to property taxes paid to your local government, and *insurance* is your homeowner's insurance policy that covers damages to the property. These items are combined into a single mortgage payment, which you pay to your lender monthly (assuming you have set up escrow, as described below).

Escrow

An escrow account is like a savings account, set up by your mortgage company. Each month, when you make your mortgage payment, 1/12 of your annual homeowner's insurance premium, and property taxes are set aside so that funds are available to pay the bills when they become due. It's your lender's way of ensuring that your taxes and insurance are paid on time.

> *If you're putting less than 20% down on your mortgage, an escrow account is required. Otherwise, it's optional.*

Be aware that some lenders charge a fee to waive escrow (0.25% of the loan amount). Also know that your monthly PITI payment may change each year if tax assessments and insurance premiums rise or fall, resulting in escrow surpluses (refunds) or shortages (requiring additional payments).

Prepaids

"Prepaids" are upfront payments made at closing for future housing expenses, such as property taxes, homeowners' insurance, and interest. At closing, your lender will collect interest from your closing date until your first mortgage payment. You will also pay not only your annual insurance premium to insure the property for the first year, but also two months' reserves (taxes and insurance) to set up your escrow account. This reserve ensures funds are available to cover unexpected increases in taxes or insurance premiums, preventing a negative balance.

PAR Rate

The "par" rate is the baseline rate offered by a lender, before any credits are given or points are paid. It is based on your financial profile and market conditions; what's par today won't be par tomorrow. Note that a *true* par rate has zero points and zero credits. In reality, most rate sheets show par rates that fall close to zero, but not exactly zero. To get to the true par rate, a small credit or point is required.

Mortgage Brokers vs. Banks vs. Online Lenders

When shopping for a loan, you can use a mortgage broker or a direct lender, such as a bank or online lender. What follows is a simplified overview of the differences between them.

Mortgage Brokers

Mortgage *Brokers* hire Mortgage *Loan Officers (MLO)* to sell loans to consumers. Brokers have dozens of accounts with *wholesale lenders*, who are the actual sources of funds. These wholesale lenders provide mortgage brokers with their wholesale rate sheets; the mortgage broker adds their cost and profit to the wholesale rates to create their retail rate sheet. Mortgage loan officers use the retail rate sheet to sell loans to consumers.

Mortgage loan officers know the wholesale marketplace well. They track which lenders offer the best rates and lowest fees, as well as those that offer discounts or unique products, such as down payment assistance, hero loans, or first-time homebuyer programs. They shop and compare wholesale interest rates for you from all kinds of banks and lending institutions. In fact, they can often get you a better price than if you went to the bank directly. It's not uncommon for a broker to sell you a Wells Fargo loan, for example, at a lower price than you could get if you went directly to Wells Fargo!

Because there is less bureaucracy with a mortgage broker, their process is generally more streamlined and efficient (assuming an equal level of competency) than working with a bank. And it's a much more personal experience. More often than not, you're dealing directly with the loan officer and their processor, not the underwriter, closer, funder, or other members of their team. You have someone who knows you in your corner, ensuring you're getting the best possible rates and service.

On the downside, commission structures vary widely from one broker to the next, so it's important to shop more than one broker. The experience and professionalism of brokers vary, so a poor choice can lead to subpar service. And – just like hiring a Realtor – choosing the right broker means finding someone you can trust to protect your interests and put your needs ahead of their own.

Banks

Bank of America, Wells Fargo, and Chase are examples of big, national banks that can loan you money to buy a house. Big banks have the capital to permanently keep your mortgage in their portfolio, if they choose. You get a mortgage from Chase and make your payments to Chase until the loan is paid off. Banks only sell their own loans, which means they offer only a few products, whereas a mortgage broker has access to dozens or hundreds of loan programs and lenders. Bank fees and rates are usually fixed, so there's little to no room for negotiation.

When dealing with a bank, the loan officers, processors, underwriters, and funders all work for the same company. The loan officer sells you the loan and passes your file to the processor. Once processed, your loan is sent to underwriting for approval. If approved, the file moves to the closing department. If not, it's sent back to the processor. It's an assembly line with greater margins of error, less efficiency, and less accountability. Although they are somewhat better to deal with than in years past, banks have a reputation for late closings, expensive loans, unskilled and unlicensed loan officers, and unhappy clients.

Buyers mistakenly assume that because they have their checking and savings accounts with a particular bank, they will get better pricing and qualify more easily for a loan. That's not true. Banks typically sell conforming loans and are subject to the same rules and regulations as all other lenders. They may offer you an incentive to get a loan through them, but the incentives are usually small, and they take back the incentive by rolling the financial equivalent into the backend of the loan.

In my area, many listing agents view offers from buyers who use a bank as their lender less favorably, and I often agree with their reasoning. While a small bank or a broker can close a transaction in 3 or 4 weeks, big banks often take longer and miss the closing date. Their loan officers are often untrained, unlicensed order-takers who are not qualified to provide buyers with financial advice. The loan files move — slowly and inaccurately — from department to department. If the underwriter is out sick, the file sits on their desk until they return. Dealing with large banks can, in my opinion, add unnecessary stress to the transaction.

Small, regional banks and credit unions, by contrast, don't always have the long-term funds available to keep your loans for very long. They issue mortgages that conform to industry standards and sell them to investors almost immediately, locking in their profits. Loan officers who work for brokers or small banks can be far more knowledgeable and service-oriented, in my experience (it's hit or miss). I usually have someone local to call if there's a problem that needs to be resolved. The loan officer is our point of contact throughout the process and works hard to keep their clients happy and maintain a good reputation. The same isn't true with a big bank, where the file is passed from department to department.

Online Lenders

An online lender provides loans entirely online. Unlike banks, they don't have physical locations, so their overhead is lower. Applications, approvals, and funding are all handled online via websites or apps, eliminating the need for in-person visits. Most online lenders operate like banks, funding loans with their own capital and offering a limited number of loan programs. Their shtick? Speed and price. The problem? There are several.

First, most of their perceived benefits are just marketing gimmicks. When they offer "fast approvals," they mean initial automated underwriting approval. Or fast *pre*-approvals.

> *All loan officers, regardless of whether they work for a bank, broker, or online lender, take their loan applications online, have encrypted portals for you to upload documents, and can have your initial underwriting approval within minutes.*

Quick approvals are great for pre-approval purposes, but it will take 2-4 weeks before you're "cleared to close" and can sign your closing papers. To reach the closing table, you need an appraisal (unless a waiver is approved), a survey, title work, inspections, etc. So, when a lender's claim to fame is quick approvals, don't be too impressed. It's just marketing. Loan approval does not mean you're cleared to close.

Next, online lenders also talk endlessly about pricing, claiming the lowest rates and the cheapest fees. They advertise their lowest rate, which usually requires the borrower to pay points. Or they promise no closing costs when, in reality, the closing costs are built into the price of the loan. They even quote prices based on qualifying terms that most buyers can't match. If they can get you to visit their site, they can spam you nonstop and hope to sell you a loan. Or hazard insurance. Or mortgage insurance. Once you click, you're no longer a borrower; you're a lead whose name will be sold and shared over and over and over again. Forever. Until you die, and probably a few years after.

Lenders can advertise whatever they want, but loan prices are highly individualized, so their ads are meaningless. Pricing is *always* based on the borrower's financial profile and the lender's desired profit margin on the loan.

> *To quote an arbitrary rate based on a financial profile that most people don't have is disingenuous, but not illegal.*

I have mixed feelings about online lenders. Occasionally, I review pricing for a buyer, and the prices are almost too good to be true. More often, though, the interest rate and fees are about the same or a bit higher than what a good broker can find. And, occasionally, their pricing is so off-the-charts expensive that I can't believe my eyes.

But the biggest problem I have with online lenders is that they operate like banks or big corporations. Your file gets passed from one department to the next, like an assembly line. Their loan officers aren't financial advisors; they are order takers. You're assigned a loan officer at random after you complete a loan application, and you have no idea if they are competent and capable of providing advice you can trust. They review your loan application, fill in any missing data, and send it through their computer system. Then, the robots take over. You may never talk to the same person twice; there's no one looking out for your best interests. What if interest rates drop? Will they float you to the lower rate? Will they help you decide when to lock your rate? It's just you vs. the machine. And since many online lenders don't play nicely with Realtors, it is much harder for me – and my clients – to monitor the loan's progress.

> *Automation can be a great thing, but it's far better for them than you.*

How Lenders Make Money

Lenders like to pretend that a mortgage isn't a commodity like a pair of shoes – but it is. Frank's Sporting Goods, for example, buys its shoes either directly from manufacturers or through wholesalers. They add their expenses and desired profit to their cost to determine the price they ultimately charge their customers. Loans work the same way.

Wholesale interest rate + closing costs + lender's profit = Borrower's Price

Let's look at these items individually.

The *wholesale interest rate* can vary – a little or a lot – from lender to lender. Larger, higher-volume brokerages can negotiate better pricing with their wholesale lender partners; banks and online direct lenders adjust their "par" (baseline) rate in line with market conditions. But for the most part, the wholesale rate is not very negotiable.

In-house closing costs, such as an origination fee, processing fee, or admin fee, may be a little negotiable, but *third-party closing costs* are not. The appraisal, survey, title search, inspector, escrow, credit report, and flood certification are all examples of third-party closing costs. The good news? It's no longer permissible for lenders to overcharge you for the cost of the appraisal, for example, and pocket the difference, and they can't charge you for services that weren't performed. These practices were very common prior to the 2007 mortgage crisis and the advent of the Consumer Financial Protection Bureau (CFPB), but new regulations have all but eliminated those fraudulent activities.

The *lender's profit* is paid on the front end as an origination fee, on the back end as a yield spread premium (YSP), or both! *The lender's profit might be negotiable.* If the lender wants a profit of 3%, for example, they could:

- Give you their wholesale interest rate and charge you a 3% origination fee upfront.
- Give you a 0% origination fee and get paid 3% on the backend in YSP.
- Charge you a 1.5% origination fee upfront AND collect 1.5% in yield spread on the backend.
- Use any combination of origination fees and yield spreads that totals their desired profit.

Remember that you don't know how much profit a lender wishes to make, and – just like Frank's Sporting Goods – they have no obligation, nor do they intend to share this information with you. Why should they? Like any other business, lenders want to make money, and they are entitled to do so. They *might* be willing to cut profits to make a deal work. A mortgage loan officer (broker) *may* reduce their commission and work for a little less to win your business. They might set their compensation at 2.5% to undercut the loan officer down the street who earns 2.75%. They could waive an in-house fee, such as an administrative fee. More than likely, they have a little room for negotiation built in. If you want to negotiate a better deal, focus on origination charges, but keep in mind that if they take it off the front, they might add it to the back.

Structuring Your Loan

Now that you know how lenders get paid, you can use this information to structure your loan in a way that best works for you.

Buyer Paid Closing Costs

Borrower paid means you, the borrower, pay your own closing costs, either in cash at closing or through a seller contribution. Doing so enables you to get the lowest possible interest rate offered by this lender. Your list of closing costs will usually include an origination fee and an itemization of other closing costs for processing, underwriting, credit reports, and related services. We'll take a closer look at Loan Estimates and comparison shopping later in this chapter.

If your goal is to secure the lowest interest rate, you have enough cash for your down payment and closing costs, and you plan to own the property for a long time, this is the better option. Not only will your mortgage payments be lower, but you'll also pay far less interest in the long run.

Lender Paid Closing Costs

Lender paid closing costs, or lender credits, allow you to reduce or eliminate upfront closing fees in exchange for a higher mortgage interest rate. This strategy minimizes the cash required at closing, making homeownership more accessible to more people. Note that lender credits can *only* be applied to bona fide closing costs and prepaids, and not for your down payment.

> *If you prefer to put down less money, don't have funds to cover your closing costs, or plan to be in the home for a shorter period, it might make more sense to have the lender cover your fees. Your interest rate and mortgage payment will be higher, but you'll need to take less money to the closing table.*

To help you understand lender credits, let's look at a real rate sheet.

More Rates

Rate	Discount Pts.	Mo. P+I ▾
5.125%	3.128% ($14,076)	$2,450
5.250%	2.568% ($11,556)	$2,485
5.375%	2.017% ($9,077)	$2,520
5.500%	1.402% ($6,309)	$2,555
5.625%	0.926% ($4,167)	$2,590
5.750%	0.304% ($1,368)	$2,626
5.875%	-0.193% (-$869)	$2,662
5.990%	-0.476% (-$2,142)	$2,695
6.000%	-0.516% (-$2,322)	$2,698
6.125%	-0.958% (-$4,311)	$2,734
6.250%	-1.133% (-$5,099)	$2,771
6.375%	-1.492% (-$6,714)	$2,807

In this case, the closest to the "par" or "baseline" rate is 5.875% (highlighted). If you agree to a 5.875% interest rate, you'll get a *lender credit* of $869. If you want to buy down the rate to 5.25%, you'll *pay* 2.568% in discount points, or $11,556, in addition to your other closing costs. If you want to keep your out-of-pocket expense as low as possible, you can agree to an interest rate of 6.375% and *receive* a rebate of $6,714, which you'll use to cover some of your closing costs. Work with your lender to choose the option that's best for you.

Comparison Shopping

Following the 2007 housing crisis and mortgage catastrophe, new regulations were introduced to ensure buyers understand their loan commitments. TILA-RESPA Integrated Disclosures (TRID), also known as the "Know Before You Owe" rules, require lenders to disclose certain information to borrowers. TRID was created to make it easier for borrowers to shop for a mortgage and harder for lenders to take advantage of confused borrowers.

At its core, TRID requires lenders to provide the buyer with a Loan Estimate within 3 days of application, guarantee the fees on the Loan Estimate, and deliver the Closing Disclosure 3 days prior to closing.

The law *requires* that when a borrower sends a lender the following information, either via their loan application or via email, the lender MUST send them a Loan Estimate within three business days:

- Your full name(s)
- Your monthly income(s)
- Your Social Security number(s)
- The property address
- The loan amount
- The property value or sales price

Providing them with all this information triggers the RESPA (mortgage law) requirement that the lender provide you with a formal Loan Estimate and all the price guarantees that come along with it. It's not optional. It's not negotiable. It's the law.

Simple enough, right? Not so fast. TRID has created as many problems as it's solved.

First, when you go under contract to buy a home, you usually can't wait three days to receive a Loan Estimate and pick a lender. Collecting Loan Estimates before you have a house isn't possible, since a property address is required to "trigger TRID" and receive an LE; the three-day delivery period, therefore, may work for the lender but isn't practical in the real world of homebuying.

Second, TRID regulations have created significant headaches for lenders, and most want to delay issuing a Loan Estimate as long as possible, and even then, only want to do so after you've committed to working with them. So, instead of providing an official Loan Estimate, most lenders only give you a quote on an "Initial Fees Worksheet" or a "Financing Scenario" instead of the Loan Estimate, which commits them to the prices that they quote. You're expected to trust that the lender will deliver on its promises.

> *By providing you with an "Initial Fees Worksheet" or a "Financing Scenario," the lender is giving you a price without triggering TRID and providing you with all the consumer protection you're entitled to.*

Think about that. The borrower wants to follow the consumer advice available online and that of the Consumer Financial Protection Bureau (CFPB). Even more ironic is that at the top of EVERY "Initial Fees Worksheet" or "Financing Scenario" is a consumer alert that states, "Your actual rate, payment, and costs could be higher. Get an official loan estimate before selecting a loan." Yet when a borrower requests an LE, the lender won't comply without a fight.

Since these laws went into effect, I've heard a variety of explanations for their lack of compliance. Here are some of them:

- "We don't send a Loan Estimate until we have a complete loan application, a copy of the sales contract, and an intent to proceed." In other words, after you commit to working with us, we'll tell you how much it costs.
- "We require full docs and payment for the appraisal before we send out a Loan Estimate." (Note: It is illegal for a lender to

require you to pay for anything more than a credit report before sending you a Loan Estimate.)

- "That's not the way we do things. At this company, disclosures are sent out by the disclosures team. I can't send your file to them until you have signed an Intent to Proceed."
- "You'll receive our Loan Estimate from my processor in a few days."

And, when the issue is forced, buyers have been given Loan Estimates that are incomplete and highly inaccurate, rendering them all but useless. Key information is deliberately excluded so that the lender is committed to nothing, or they ghost the borrower altogether and move on to the next one. One thing is for certain: Lenders do not want to "trigger TRID" and provide the Loan Estimates needed to shop around.

I've spent *years* trying to understand what was happening behind the scenes in the mortgage industry. Literally years. And I'm not the only one. A quick search on Reddit or similar sites reveals the frustration amongst borrowers and agents alike. Helping my clients shop for the best financing was no easier than it had been before the new TRID laws. Consumer advocates like me have spent decades trying to improve the buyer's experience and to minimize their risk. It took a real estate crash and a subprime mortgage crisis to finally implement positive changes, but they haven't helped. If anything, it made things more confusing for the borrower and more costly and frustrating for the lender.

I finally decided that the best way to understand the mortgage industry was to work in it. I earned my license and began a secondary career as a mortgage loan officer.

The Idiot Who "Triggered TRID"

I signed up with my first mortgage broker shortly after receiving my mortgage license. Much to my surprise, loan officers with this firm weren't allowed to generate Loan Estimates. They accepted loan applications and sent financing scenarios, but beyond that, the borrower was referred to a different department that generated the LEs and took over the transaction. My second broker operated similarly, except all they wanted me to do was get the loan application and send the file up the food chain. I wasn't even supposed to provide pricing. I can't in good conscience represent my clients that way.

It was my third mortgage broker who operated much like I operate my real estate brokerage. Loan officers act as the borrower's fiduciary. Their job is to hold the borrower's hand and be involved in every step of the process. The staff and owners are smart and experienced, and they uphold the highest ethical standards. Plus, their pricing was more than fair. They give me the freedom to set my own commission rather than demand the industry-standard (but negotiable) rate. I had found my mortgage home. This was the right place, I believed, to learn the mortgage industry from the ground up.

The first thing I learned is that even the most honest, law-abiding mortgage brokers like mine avoid "triggering TRID," or the requirement to deliver a Loan Estimate within 3 days. I'm a play-by-the-rules kind of person, so I triggered TRID early and often, not aware of the processes and legal consequences of doing so. I was shamed more than once for doing it, usually by third-party processors. My name is Alysse Musgrave, and I am the idiot who "triggered TRID."

As it turns out, there are complex regulatory rules and guidelines that brokers must follow to comply with the laws and regulations set by the Consumer Financial Protection Bureau; the details of those guidelines are well beyond the scope of this book (and often beyond my comprehension), but I can tell you that fines for noncompliance are steep and the consequences severe. Triggering TRID creates a lot of work for those working behind the scenes. The 3-day delivery requirement clock starts, and audit trails are initiated. A long list of very specific items must be documented in the event of an audit, regardless of whether the borrower ultimately worked with me as their loan officer. It's a lot of paperwork and monitoring, sometimes for naught.

I also learned that it's hard to deliver a 100% accurate Loan Estimate without involving the title company, real estate agents, and others. Title companies, for example, usually don't get involved in the transaction until later in the buying cycle, and asking them to get involved before a borrower has signed an Intent to Proceed (a letter from the borrower confirming that they want to move forward with a particular lender) is a big ask and a potential waste of time. I would be claiming those borrowers as my clients before I was authorized to do so. In addition, Buyers are expected to finalize financing while conducting home inspections and negotiating repairs, so seller credits are not yet known. For these reasons (and others), we're required to estimate certain fees and eliminate others, which can confuse the borrower when their Loan Estimate doesn't match their Closing Disclosure.

Lastly, as a Mortgage Loan Officer, I am responsible for ensuring the fees I disclose on a Loan Estimate are accurate. It's not a problem if I disclose a fee that is higher than you ultimately pay. If, for example, I disclose an appraisal fee of $1,000, but the actual charge is $600, you'll only pay $600. However, if I disclose an appraisal fee of $600 and the cost is $1,000, *I* am required to pay the $400 difference. Some fees, such as lender fees, have a "zero tolerance" policy, meaning I must get it right or cover the difference. Other fees, such as third-party closing costs, have a 10% tolerance, meaning I can be off by up to 10% before I must make up the difference on my client's behalf.

> *Since some of the fees disclosed on the LE are binding and any shortages are charged to the loan officer or lender, it is important to lenders that they get the math right. Can you blame them? But it's hard to do too early in the buying cycle.*

Lenders and their loan officers have a dilemma. If their quote is too high to protect themselves against tolerance issues, their pricing isn't competitive. If they quote too low, they risk tolerance issues and may be forced to pay the buyer's fees. It's not easy to find the right balance. And the lender's dilemma becomes a problem for borrowers as they shop for loans.

The Problem With TRID

So, what does this all mean? It means that the Department of Housing and Urban Development's (HUD) well-intentioned initiatives to make loan shopping easier for borrowers have failed, at least to a certain degree.

From the lender's perspective, TRID is far too complex and rigid. It leads to delays in closing, expensive tolerance cures, and high rates of technical errors. A missing hyphen or improper expense label can cause investors to reject loans. There are over 2,000+ pages of rules that lenders must follow. The administrative burden of maintaining proper documentation is high, and there is increased stress and cost due to the potential for legal liability and regulatory penalties.

For the borrower, there's still no easy, standardized way to compare lenders' quotes, as you'll see in the next section.

Shopping for a loan should be about the math and require no element of trust. That's not the case. Borrowers are forced to trust the lender will deliver what is promised based on non-standard quotes and procedures.

Home Loan Options

Not all home loans are the same. Knowing which loan is most appropriate for your situation prepares you to talk to lenders and get the best deal. Loans have three elements: Loan type, loan term, and interest rate type. Each of these elements is discussed in this section.

Loan Types

Loan types are categorized by loan size and whether they are part of a government program. Your choice affects how much you need to put down, the cost of the loan (including the interest rate and mortgage insurance), and how much you can borrow.

FHA Financing

FHA is a government-insured mortgage program, meaning the government guarantees the loan if the borrower defaults. This type of financing was part of the government's initiative to encourage homeownership. The credit requirements are much more relaxed, and the interest rate is lower since a government-backed mortgage means no risk to the lender. The minimum down payment for an FHA loan is just 3.5 percent of the purchase price, and FHA accepts gifted funds toward the down payment or closing costs.

The FHA program is increasingly popular since it is easier to qualify for than a conventional mortgage. FHA, however, can be more expensive in the long run than conventional financing, largely due to the required mortgage insurance premiums. FHA also requires the property to meet certain standards for loan approval, and it's not uncommon for the lender to require repairs before closing.

Mortgage Insurance Premium (MIP)

Mortgage insurance is a policy that protects lenders against borrower defaults on loans. FHA loans require *two* distinct mortgage insurance premiums for most borrowers. The first is the Upfront Mortgage Insurance Premium (UFMIP), a percentage of your total loan amount (approximately 1.75 percent). It can be paid in cash at closing or can be rolled into the loan amount. On a $300,000 house, that's $5,250! A portion of the fee is refundable when you refinance into another FHA loan within three years but, beyond that, it's wasted money.

The second type of mortgage insurance is called monthly MIP (Mortgage Insurance Premium). MIP premiums are paid as part of your monthly mortgage payments. In years past, MIP could be cancelled once the borrower had roughly 20% equity in the home, either through appreciation or principal reduction. *Those days are gone.* In 2013, the rules changed, and FHA borrowers who put less than 10% down will have to pay the MIP premium for the life of the loan. I'll repeat this statement for emphasis.

> *FHA borrowers who put down less than 10% will have to pay the annual MIP for the life of the loan. Ouch.*

Remarkably, borrowers with credit scores between 500 and 579 can qualify for FHA financing with a 10% down payment. If your credit score is 580 or higher, you only need 3.5% down. In either case, your closing costs can be paid by the lender, the seller, or rolled into the loan.

FHA is a great option for some borrowers purchasing a home in reasonably good condition. But if you have a credit score of 680 or higher and have little money in the bank, a better loan for you might be Conventional 97, discussed below.

Conventional Financing

A conventional loan is a loan not insured by the government; the lender bears the risk of losing money if the borrower defaults on the mortgage. Conventional mortgages are for those borrowers with better credit; credit scores need to be in the 680-plus range. Expect to put down between 3 percent and 20 percent when you purchase a home using a conventional mortgage.

Private Mortgage Insurance (PMI)

Most lenders require Private Mortgage Insurance (PMI) when the buyer puts down less than 20% of the home's value upon purchase. PMI allows borrowers to make smaller down payments and enables them to buy a home sooner since they don't need a huge down payment to qualify. Unlike an FHA loan, which requires two kinds of mortgage insurance, there is no upfront premium with a conventional loan. In addition, PMI can be cancelled when the homeowner has sufficient equity in the property (usually 20-22 percent), either through appreciation or principal reduction.

Conventional 97

The Conventional 97 program requires a minimum 3 percent down payment, based on the lower of the home's appraised value or purchase price. On a $150,000 house, this translates to a down payment of $4,500 (3%), compared with $5,250 for an FHA loan (3.5%). In addition to the other benefits of a conventional loan mentioned above (no upfront premium and the ability to cancel PMI once 20% equity is reached), down payment funds can be gifted by third parties. If you're a first-time homebuyer, you may be required to take an online homebuyer responsibility course to qualify. If you have a credit score of at least 680 and the required down payment, the Conventional 97 might be a good loan for you.

VA Loans

A VA loan is a mortgage benefit for eligible Veterans, service members, and surviving spouses that helps them buy a home with no down payment and no private mortgage insurance (PMI). VA loans require a one-time VA funding fee, unless the borrower qualifies for an exemption. The home purchased must meet VA minimum property requirements for value and condition. Because VA loans are backed by the government, interest rates tend to be lower than with conventional financing.

Investor Financing

An investment loan funds income generating assets such as rental properties or fix-and-flip projects, allowing investors to purchase property for profit rather than personal use. These loans require higher down payments and credit scores and come with greater asset reserve requirements than primary mortgages. Interest rates are higher for investment loans to compensate the lender for the increased risk, and a market rental analysis is often required as part of the appraisal process.

USDA/Rural Housing Loans

USDA loans are insured by the Department of Agriculture. Their most notable feature is their option for "no money down" or "100% financing." The purpose of the loan is to spur the development of rural areas, and both the property and the buyer must qualify for USDA financing. Beyond that, they are very similar to other types of loans.

Except for VA financing, USDA loans are really the only source of no money down financing these days. Why? Because when a homeowner doesn't have any skin in the game (home equity), the chance they will walk away from their mortgage and go into foreclosure is much higher. Most lenders are no longer comfortable with that level of risk. In addition, no money down means the buyer is rolling their closing costs and mortgage insurance into the loan. Even though interest rates for USDA loans are lower than those for FHA or Conventional loans, with no down payment and added loan fees, monthly PITI payments can still be quite high. If the homeowner can no longer afford their payments and doesn't have enough equity in the property to cover their selling expenses, they are stuck. They have no choice but to walk away from their mortgage or dig into their retirement account.

Loan Terms

The loan term refers to the time you have to repay your loan. Longer terms mean lower monthly payments but more total interest; shorter terms mean higher payments but less overall interest.

30-Year Mortgage

A 30-year fixed rate mortgage is the most popular home loan. It features consistent monthly payments over 360 months with a locked interest rate for the entire term. Monthly payments are lower than those for 15- or 20-year options. This increases your buying power but results in higher total interest costs. Because more of the early payments go toward interest rather than principal, equity builds up more slowly than in a 15-year mortgage.

The lower mortgage payment associated with a 30-year loan helps borrowers qualify for a more expensive home since their debt-to-income ratios are also lower. It is ideal for first time homebuyers, those on a strict budget, or anyone looking to maximize their monthly cash flow.

15-Year Mortgage

A 15-year mortgage is an amortized loan repaid in 15 years, offering significantly lower interest rates (as much as 0.55% lower) and faster equity growth than a 30-year loan, but with higher, less flexible monthly payments. They are ideal for homeowners focused on paying off debt quickly, saving on total interest, and securing a stable, lower, fixed rate. Because the loan is repaid in half the time, monthly payments are substantially higher, which may strain your budget and reduce financial flexibility. Lenders require higher credit scores (often 740+) and lower debt-to-income (DTI) ratios (typically under 50%) because of the higher payments.

Interest Rate Type

Fixed or adjustable refers to the interest rate, which can either remain the same throughout the life of the loan or change periodically. Fixed and adjustable rates are discussed below.

Fixed-Rate Mortgages

A fixed-rate mortgage has an interest rate that never changes. This means, unlike an adjustable rate mortgage, you are protected from higher monthly mortgage payments if interest rates suddenly rise. If mortgage rates drop, however, you do not benefit from the lower rate unless you refinance. The vast majority of homebuyers prefer the predictability of a fixed-rate mortgage.

Adjustable Rate Mortgages

ARMs (Adjustable Rate Mortgages) are attractive to some because the initial rate is low, which allows the borrower to qualify for a larger loan. They are risky because your interest rate (and therefore your mortgage payment) changes frequently over the life of the loan. Some are structured so that interest rates can more than *double* in just a few years. If you don't plan to live in a property long enough for the rates to rise, then an ARM might be a good choice. Otherwise, stick with a fixed rate mortgage.

Shopping for a Loan

After you have found a house, contact several lenders (including the one who wrote your pre-approval letter) and ask for a Loan Estimate. Since rates change daily, and sometimes hourly, be sure to contact lenders on the same day and at roughly the same time. You also need to compare apples to apples when you get your Loan Estimates. Don't compare a 15-year ARM with a 30-year fixed, for example.

Pay attention to the level of service you receive. Did they return your call or email promptly? If you completed an online form, did you receive anything beyond an automated response? Did they offer you financial advice or just try to sell you a loan? Did they ask you about your financial goals and act as an advisor, not a salesperson? Is this person someone you'd like to work with for the next four to six weeks? Eliminate lenders whose demeanor and skills don't impress you. Send the others the following information, either via their loan application (preferred) or via email:

- Your full name(s)
- Your monthly income(s)
- Your Social Security number(s)
- The property address
- The loan amount
- The property value or sales price

Providing them with *all* this information triggers the requirement to deliver a formal Loan Estimate (LE) within three days. Will you receive a Loan Estimate without a fight? From what I hear from my clients, for every five lenders they speak to, one or two will send a Loan Estimate. The rest send a quote in a different format, discussed in detail later in this chapter.

The Loan Estimate (LE) – A Detailed Look

The Consumer Financial Protection Bureau (CFPB) requires easy-to-understand mortgage disclosure forms that clearly lay out the terms of a mortgage for a homebuyer. The "Know Before You Owe" mortgage forms, known as the Loan Estimate (LE) and Closing Disclosure (CD), replaced the Good Faith Estimate (GFE) and HUD-1 in October 2015. These forms were created to help consumers understand their options, choose the deal that's best for them, and avoid costly surprises at the closing table.

The new Loan Estimate document is so well written that it needs no explanation. Really. It is just three pages long (see below).

- The first page lists the borrower(s), loan terms, projected monthly payments, total estimated closing costs, and the total estimated cash needed to close.
- The second page breaks down the closing costs in more detail, including prepaid and escrowed amounts, as well as the cash needed to close.
- The third page includes a summary of loan costs over five years, along with required disclosures regarding the delivery of a copy of an appraisal to the borrower, whether the loan is assumable, whether homeowners' insurance is required, late payment fee information, and whether loan servicing may be transferred. The third page also contains a signature block for consumers to confirm receipt of the disclosure.

Easy, right? You would think. The Loan Estimate template is a well-written and easy-to-understand document, yes. The CFPB did a great job creating this form. But without standardized and enforceable ways to label fees and calculate the APR, comparison shopping can be an exercise in futility. Let's try to make sense out of the insanity.

Start by downloading and printing a marked-up copy of the sample loan estimate by visiting http://BAH8.net.

There are only THREE sections you should focus on when comparing loan estimates: Section A: Origination Charges, Section B: Services You Cannot Shop For, and Section J: Lender Credits, all highlighted in the sample loan estimate on the next page.

Section A: Origination Charges

Origination charges are paid directly to the lender and are listed in section A. This includes underwriting, processing, administration, application fees, points, loan officer commissions, and other fees.

Lenders are free to disclose their origination charges however they want. They can bundle many fees into a single origination fee, or they can claim no origination fee and hide the costs in the interest rate. When a buyer negotiates an origination fee, they can reduce it, waive it, or waive it up front and recoup it on the back end.

The point is that the lender has complete control over the fees in Section A, but there is a "zero tolerance" policy for items listed there: fees cannot increase, and new fees cannot be added once the loan is locked.

Section B: Third-Party Fees

Section B contains third-party, non-negotiable fees required to close the loan. These are services you cannot shop for. You can't pick your appraiser, order your own credit report, or order a flood certificate. The lender collects fees for these services from you, and the vendor is paid at closing. Fees in the section are subject to a 10% tolerance limit, meaning they cannot increase by more than 10% in aggregate on the final closing disclosure. If they do, the lender or loan officer must cover the difference.

Section J: Lender Credits

Lenders use credits or rebates to offset closing costs and to reduce a borrower's cash at closing requirement. In exchange for the lender credit, you pay a higher interest rate than you would have received with the same lender for the same kind of loan without lender credits. The more lender credits you receive, the higher your rate will be.

Changes in income, sales price, loan program, or locking your rate can trigger a new Loan Estimate, rendering the original obsolete. That means if you don't lock your interest rate, if you buy a different house, or if there is a change to your qualifications, the lender can issue a new Loan Estimate with the new pricing, rendering your original quote void.

Closing Cost Details

Loan Costs

A. Origination Charges	**$6,590**
% of Loan Amount (Points)	
Origination Fee	$4,500
Processing Fee	$995
Underwriting Fee	$1,095

B. Services You Cannot Shop For	**$752**
Appraisal Fee	$600
Credit Report Fee	$75
Flood Certification Fee	$7
Tax Service Fee	$70

C. Services You Can Shop For	**$3,870**
Survey Fee	$350
Title - Document Prep Fee	$4
Title - Lender's Endorsement Fee	$204
Title - Lender's Title Insurance	$2,677
Title - Settlement Or Closing Fee	$550
Title - Tax Certificate/Guaranty Fee	$85

D. TOTAL LOAN COSTS (A + B +C)	**$11,212**

Other Costs

E. Taxes and Other Government Fees	**$227**
Recording Fees and Other Taxes	$227
Transfer Taxes	

F. Prepaids	**$4,069**
Homeowner's Insurance Premium (12 months)	$1,775
Mortgage Insurance Premium (months)	
Prepaid Interest ($71.88 per day for 2 days @ 5.75%)	$144
Property Taxes (3 months)	$2,150

G. Initial Escrow Payment at Closing		**$2,782**
Homeowner's Insurance	$147.92 per month for 3 mo.	$444
Mortgage Insurance	$93.75 per month for 2 mo.	$188
Property Taxes	$716.67 per month for 3 mo.	$2,150

H. Other	**$588**
Title - Owner's Title Insurance (Optional)	$363
Tx Attorney Fee	$225

I. TOTAL OTHER COSTS (E + F + G +H)	**$7,666**
J. TOTAL CLOSING COSTS	**$18,878**
D + I	$18,878
Lender Credits	$7,666

Calculating Cash to Close

Total Closing Costs (J)	$18,878
Closing Costs Financed (Paid from your Loan Amount)	$0
Down Payment/Funds from Borrower	$50,000
Deposit	-$5,000
Funds for Borrower	$0
Seller Credits	-$2,500
Adjustments and Other Credits	-$500
Estimated Cash to Close	$60,878

Comparing Loan Estimates

If you are under the assumption that a lender wants to make it easy for you to shop around, you are dead wrong. It's quite the opposite. Lenders shop each other constantly and adjust their quotes to win the business. That doesn't make them evil; these aren't non-profit organizations. But – as a consumer – you do need to educate yourself on how to get the best deal. Follow the tips below.

Annual Percentage Rate (APR)

The interest rate is the annual cost of borrowing money. The Annual Percentage Rate (APR) reflects the interest rate PLUS other fees, such as points, origination fees, and other charges. As part of TRID, lenders are required to disclose the APR to make it easier for borrowers to compare loan programs and shop lenders. The CFPB and other resources advise borrowers to use the APR to identify the lowest cost loan; the lower the APR, the cheaper the loan. Unfortunately, it won't work. Here's why.

Lenders and loan officers are free to choose which fees to include in the APR. Some lenders over-disclose and include a "worst case" APR in their initial Loan Estimates, then try to come in lower with the Closing Disclosure. This protects them when one state or wholesale lender requires fees to be included in the APR that another doesn't, but it hurts them when buyers compare their APR to a lender with different policies. *It ultimately makes their loan appear more expensive than it is.*

Other companies show the lowest legally possible APR in the initial LE to make their loans appear cheaper than they really are. How can a company lower APR? They can reduce the number of days of prepaid interest to one rather than using the actual figure. They can mark certain fees payable in cash at closing rather than as part of the loan. They can rename fees so that APR fees appear to be non-APR fees. *These tricks can make a more expensive loan appear to have a lower APR.* I can't speak to the legality of these practices since I'm not an attorney, but it's icky at the very least.

How to Use the APR to Compare Mortgages

Since you don't always know what fees the lender includes in the APR, you'll have to calculate it for yourself. Start by compiling a list of the following, using the estimates you receive from various lenders:

- Home value (usually the sales price)
- Down payment %
- Loan term – (See Loan Estimate – page 1)
- Interest rate – (See Loan Estimate page 1)
- Loan fees (see explanation below)
- Points (See Loan Estimate page 2, Section A. Use the %, not the dollar amount)
- PMI Mortgage Insurance /year (See Loan Estimate page 1, projected payments. Multiply this figure x 12 to calculate your annual premium.)

To determine which loan fees to include, use the calculation below from the sample Loan Estimate below (Figure 2):

Section A (not including points) + Section B = Total Fees
Total Fees – Lender Credits = Net Closing Costs

EXAMPLE

Section A: $4,500 + 995 + $1,095 = $6,590
Section B: $600 + $75 + $7 + $70 = $752
Totals of Sections: A + B = $7,342

Closing Cost Details

Loan Costs

A. Origination Charges	$9,164
.572% of Loan Amount (Points)	$2,574
Origination Fee	$4,500
Processing Fee	$995
Underwriting Fee	$1,095

B. Services You Cannot Shop For	$752
Appraisal Fee	$600
Credit Report Fee	$75
Flood Certification Fee	$7
Tax Service Fee	$70

C. Services You Can Shop For	$3,870
Survey Fee	$350
Title - Document Prep Fee	$4
Title - Lender's Endorsement Fee	$204
Title - Lender's Title Insurance	$2,677
Title - Settlement Or Closing Fee	$550
Title - Tax Certificate/Guaranty Fee	$85

D. TOTAL LOAN COSTS (A + B +C)	$11,212

Other Costs

E. Taxes and Other Government Fees	$227
Recording Fees and Other Taxes	$227
Transfer Taxes	

F. Prepaids	$4,062
Homeowner's Insurance Premium(12months)	$1,775
Mortgage Insurance Premium (months)	
Prepaid Interest ($71.88 per day for2days @ 5.75%)	$137
Property Taxes (3 months)	$2,150

G. Initial Escrow Payment at Closing		$2,782
Homeowner's Insurance	$147.92per month for 3 mo.	$444
Mortgage Insurance	$93.75per month for 2 mo.	$188
Property Taxes	$716.67per month for 3 mo.	$2,150

H. Other	$588
Title - Owner's Title Insurance (Optional)	$363
Tx Attorney Fee	$225

I. TOTAL OTHER COSTS (E + F + G +H)	$7,659
J. TOTAL CLOSING COSTS	$19,945
D + I	$21,445
Lender Credits	$1,500

Calculating Cash to Close

Total Closing Costs (J)	$18,878
Closing Costs Financed (Paid from your Loan Amount)	$0
Down Payment/Funds from Borrower	$50,000
Deposit	-$5,000
Funds for Borrower	$0
Seller Credits	-$2,500
Adjustments and Other Credits	-$500
Estimated Cash to Close	$60,878

Figure 2: Sample Loan Estimate

Now that you have all the figures you need, you can use a free online calculator to compute your APR. I like https://www.calculator.net/apr-calculator.html. Be sure to use the Mortgage APR calculator. Here's what it looks like, using the figures from our sample Loan Estimate:

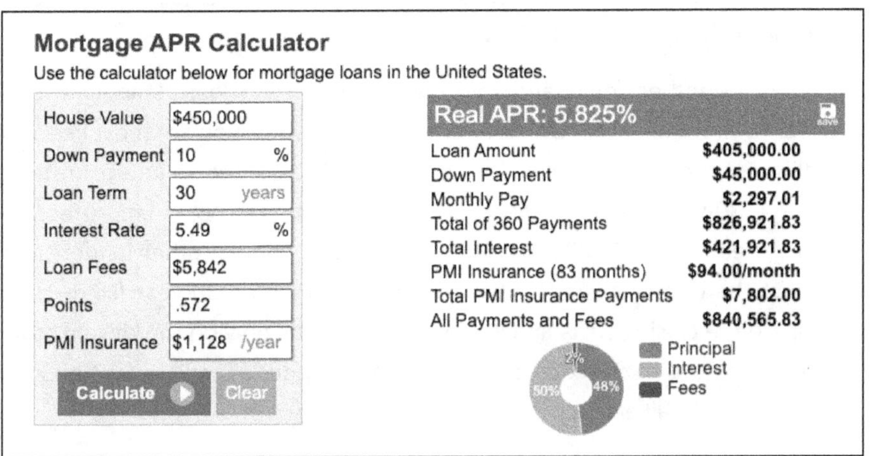

The APR of this loan is 5.825%. Use this calculator to compute the APR for all the Loan Estimates you receive; the loan with the lowest APR is the cheapest.

Calculate your five-year cost of borrowing

On average, most borrowers keep a mortgage for about five years before moving or refinancing. While your situation may differ, determining the total amount you will pay in interest and fees over five years *can* be a useful way to compare loan offers. It's imperfect because, just like the APR, you don't know which fees are used in this calculation. It's an interesting figure, though, and warrants a quick mention.

On page 3 of the Loan Estimate, locate the "In 5 years" line in the Comparisons section. The first number shows you the total dollar amount (including principal) you will pay over five years. The second number shows you the amount of principal you will have paid off after five years.

Subtract the second number from the first number, and you'll get the total amount of interest and fees you will have paid after five years. This is your five-year borrowing cost.

An Easy Way to Shop for a Loan

Here's another smart and easy way to shop for a loan. Start with one lender to determine the lowest interest rate for which you are most likely to qualify. For the sake of discussion, assume you are quoted an interest rate of 6% on a 30-year fixed mortgage with zero points, zero origination fee, no lender credits, and $4,000 in closing costs. Next, contact other lenders and request the closing costs for the same loan – 6% on a 30-year fixed. Then compare the closing costs and lender credits. Focus only on the closing costs in Sections A& B of the Loan Estimate and the Lender's Credit in Section J (as discussed in detail earlier).

Comparing closing costs is far easier when all the lenders are issuing quotes based on the same interest rate.

When You Can't Get a Loan Estimate

As we discussed earlier, the Consumer Financial Protection Bureau (CFPB) requires your lender to provide you with a Loan Estimate within three business days of receiving your application. The application must include the following information: your name(s), your income(s), your Social Security number(s) to obtain a credit report, the property address, an estimate of the property's value, and the loan amount.

As we've already established, some loan officers are unwilling to provide Loan Estimates in accordance with the CFPB's requirements. Instead, most lenders provide quotes for documents called "Initial Fee Sheets" or "Financing Scenarios".

Since you're far more likely to receive one of these documents rather than an initial Loan Estimate, it's a good idea for us to explore them together.

Initial Fees Worksheet

The example below is a well-designed and complete initial fees worksheet. You can download a copy of this document on my resources page: https://bah8.net. Notice that it mimics the Loan Estimate in that the fees are organized into the same categories as the Loan Estimate: Lender fees, Third Party fees, etc. Although the lender is not bound by the prices they quote, you should expect the fees quoted here to match the Loan Estimate they send you, if it's sent and locked on the same day. Like it? Lock it.

INITIAL FEES WORKSHEET

Your actual rate, payment and costs could be higher. Get an official Loan Estimate before choosing a loan.

Quote Number: 15710230

Preparation Date: 01/26/2026 1:34 PM CST

Loan Purpose:	Purchase	Purchase Price:	$500,000.00	Loan Amount:	$450,000.00
Property Type:	Single Family (1-4 Units)	Occupancy:	Primary Residence	No. of Units:	1
Credit Score:	Estimated	ZIP / State:	75019 / Texas	Escrow:	None Waived
Product:	30 Year CONVENTIONAL Fixed	Rate / APR:	6.250% / 6.580%	Lock Period:	30 Days

Lender Fees	$6,590.00
0.000% of Loan Amount (Points)	$0.00
Origination Fee	$4,500.00
Processing Fee	$995.00
Underwriting Fee	$1,095.00

Third Party Fees	$5,209.85
Services You Cannot Shop For	
Appraisal Fee	$600.00
Credit Report Fee	$75.00
Document Preparation Fee	$225.00
Flood Certificate Fee	$7.00

Services You Can Shop For	
Survey Fee	$350.00
Title - Document Prep Fee	$4.00
Title - Lender's Endorsement Fee	$203.85
Title - Lender's Title Insurance	$2,677.00
Title - Owner's Title Insurance (Optional)	$363.00
Title - Settlement or Closing Fee	$550.00
Title - Tax Certificate/Guaranty Fee	$85.00

Taxes and Other Government Fees	$227.00
Recording Fees - Deed	$37.00
Recording Fees - Mortgage	$145.00
Recording Fees - Other	$45.00

Prepaids and Initial Escrow Payment at Closing	$6,862.53
Prepaids	
Hazard Insurance Premium (12 Months @ $147.92)	$1,775.00
Mortgage Insurance Premium (0 Months @ $93.75)	$0.00
Prepaid Interest (2 Days @ $78.125)	$156.25
Property Taxes (3 Months @ $716.67)	$2,150.01
Supp Property Insurance Premium (0 Months @ $0.00)	$0.00

Initial Escrow Payment at Closing	
Hazard Insurance Reserve (3 Months @ $147.92)	$443.76
Mortgage Insurance Reserve (2 Months @ $93.75)	$187.50
Property Taxes (3 Months @ $716.67)	$2,150.01
Supp Property Insurance Reserve (0 Months @ $0.00)	$0.00
Aggregate Adjustment	$0.00

Estimated Proposed Monthly Housing Expense	
First Mortgage P&I	$2,770.73
Other Financing P&I	$0.00
Homeowner's Insurance	$147.92
Property Taxes	$716.67
Mortgage Insurance	$93.75
Homeowner Assn. Dues	$125.00

Estimated Funds to Close:	
Downpayment/Funds from Borrower	$50,000.00
Lender Fees	$6,590.00
Third Party Fees	$5,209.85
Taxes and Other Government Fees	$227.00
Prepaids and Initial Escrow	$6,862.53
Estimated Total Payoffs	$0.00
Funds Due from Borrower (A)	$68,889.38
Deposit	$5,000.00
Lender Credits	$6,390.00
Seller Credits	$2,500.00
Adjustments and Other Credits	$500.00
Total Credits Applied (B)	$14,390.00

Financing Scenario #1

The document below, entitled "Financing Scenario #1," is an example of an incomplete estimate. First, notice that the lender violates the Written Informational Rule that requires the lender to advise the borrower to obtain a Loan Estimate. Second, the document lumps closing costs, third-party fees like title insurance, surveys, homeowner's insurance, etc., into the category of "closing costs," making it difficult for you to differentiate between lender fees and third-party fees. Finally, the APR is not included in the document as is required by TRID. Based on this document, this is not a lender whom I would perceive to be professional and trustworthy.

FINANCING SCENARIO #1

Name of Borrowers: Mrs. Buyer — 30-yr Fixed
Property Address: 2999 Barclay Lane, Dallas, TX 75036

4.750%   Term. 360

Sales Price   292,221   Primary Loan Amount: 233,776.00

Loan Origination Fee					$	-
Loan Discount						
Appraisal Fee					$	450.00
Commitment Fee					$	55.00
Inspection Fee					$	-
Mortgage Insurance Application Fee					$	-
Assumption Fee					$	-
Tax Related Service Fee						
Underwriting Fee					$	800.00
Processing Fee					$	380.00
Courier Fee						
Flood Certification						
Lender Closing Fee						
Owner's Title Policy					$	1,506.00
Notary Fee						
Attorney's Fees					$	150.00
Lenders Title Ins.					$	270.00
Escrow Fee -Title Company					$	600.00
Tax Certificate					$	49.00
Restrictions						
Recording Fees					$	125.00
Survey					$	460.00
HOA Fees/Dues					$	2,170.00
Title Company-Courier					$	50.00
TOTAL CLOSING COSTS					**$**	**7,065.00**
Prepaid Interest	2	Days			$	67.24
UFMIP					$	-
Escrow: Homeowners Insuran	2	Months @	$61.92			$123.84
Escrow: Mortgage Insurance					$	-
Escrow: Local taxes	3	Months @	$125.00		$	375.00
Homeowners Ins- 1st year					$	743.04 (est)
TOTAL PREPAID ITEMS					**$**	**1,309.12**

Total Estimated Funds		**Total Estimated Monthly Payment**	
Sales Price	$292,221.00	Primary Principal/Interest	$ 1,219.49
Estimated Closing Costs	$ 7,065.00	HOA Dues	
Estimated Pre	$ 1,309.12	Real Estate Taxes	$125.00
Total Due	$300,595.12	Homeowners Insurance	$61.92
First Lien	233,776.00	PMI	
		Total Est Monthly Payment	$ 1,406.41
Earnest Money	$ 10,000.00		
Total Est Funds Needed to Close	**$56,819.12**		

Financing Scenario #2

The second fee worksheet is far more informative and user-friendly, but still not sufficient on its own to compare loans. It is, however, helpful if you want to explore lender paid vs. borrower paid closing costs, the effect of 10% vs. 20% down, or different loan types.

First, note that the lender complies with the Written Information Rule. The notice is posted at the top of the page, in 12-point font as required. This quote compares a 30-year fixed loan at 3.75% with one at 3.625%. The 3.75% interest rate option offers the borrower a $1,700 lender credit. Lender closing costs on this loan are simply an admin fee of $275. As such, their profit is built into the backend via the yield spread premium. It's a 97% loan-to-value loan, meaning the borrower has a 3% down payment, and the lender can lock the rate for 45 days (presumably at no cost), which is longer than a more common 30 days. The total monthly payment itemizes principal and interest, mortgage insurance, property taxes, and insurance escrows.

When comparing mortgages, compare only the principal and interest. The mortgage and homeowner's insurance figures, for example, are just estimates. A loan officer can use a low figure to make your monthly payment appear lower than it actually is.

This lender itemizes its closing costs (lender & third-party), totaling $2076.94. With a $1,700 lender credit, the borrower's closing costs are reduced to $376.94. Alternatively, the borrower could choose the lower interest rate of 3.625% with no lender credit, paying $2,076.94 at closing. The difference in payment is slightly lower at 3.625%, but the long-term savings are significant. If you plan to be in the home for more than 5 years, you have the cash on hand to cover the closing costs, it's better to pay the lower interest rate and refuse the lender credit.

Loan Proposal

Please note your actual rate, payment and costs could be higher. Get an official Loan Estimate before choosing a loan. Until you lock your rate, your interest rate, points and lender credits can change prior to closing.

Customer(s) **Sample Buyer**   Date 01/21/2020

Property   Arlington, TX 76010

	3.75	**3.625**
Purchase Price	$355,000.00	$355,000.00
Total Loan Amount	$344,350.00	$344,350.00
Interest Rate	3.750%	3.625%
Annual Percentage Rate (APR)	4.269%	4.130%
Amortization Type/Loan Term	Conf 30 Yr Fixed	Conf 30 Yr Fixed
Total Monthly Payment	$2,715.61	$2,691.28
Closing Costs to You	$376.94	$2,076.94
Points	$0.00	$0.00
Total Cash to You (from You)	($15,974.99)	($17,657.05)
Property Type	Owner Occupied	Owner Occupied
Waive Escrow	No	No
Structure	1 Unit	1 Unit
LTV%/CLTV%	97.00% / 0.00%	97.00% / 0.00%
Rate Lock	45	45
Principal and Interest	$1,594.74	$1,570.41
Mortgage Insurance	$200.87	$200.87
Property Taxes	$770.00	$770.00
Homeowner's Insurance	$150.00	$150.00
Total Monthly Payment	**$2,715.61**	**$2,691.28**
Administrative Fee	$275.00	$275.00
Third Party Fees		
Appraisal	$490.00	$490.00
Credit Report	$85.94	$85.94
Flood Certificate	$12.00	$12.00
Title Services/Title Insurance	$900.00	$900.00
Owner's Title Insurance	$160.00	$160.00
Government Recording Charges	$154.00	$154.00
Transfer Taxes	$0.00	$0.00
Condo Certificate	$0.00	$0.00
Pest Inspection Fee	$0.00	$0.00
Closing Costs	$2,076.94	$2,076.94
Paid Costs (Lender Credit)	$1,700.00	$0.00
Closing Costs to You	$376.94	$2,076.94
Daily Interest (Days)	$538.05 (15)	$520.11 (15)
Insurance (12 Months)	$1,800.00	$1,800.00
Homeowner's Insurance (Months)	$300.00 (2)	$300.00 (2)
Property Taxes (Months)	$2,310.00 (3)	$2,310.00 (3)
Total Prepaid Items	**$4,948.05**	**$4,930.11**
Summary		
Purchase Price	$355,000.00	$355,000.00
(+) Closing Costs to You	$376.94	$2,076.94
(+) Total Prepaid Items		
(+) Points	$0.00	$0.00
(+) PMI, MIP, Funding Fee		
(-) Total Loan Amount	$344,350.00	$344,350.00
(-) PMI, MIP, Funding Fee Financed	$0.00	$0.00
(-) Other Credits	$0.00	$0.00
Total Cash to You (from You)	**($15,974.99)**	**($17,657.05)**

Loan Officer (NMLS#)

Member FDIC. Equal Housing Lender

It's important to remember that these are not standardized forms! The lender may list or omit any fee they wish on these documents. If you're forced to shop for loans using an Initial Fees Worksheet or Financing Scenario, insist on a Loan Estimate before you proceed.

Your Loan Step-by-Step

While shopping for a loan, you've more than likely completed multiple loan applications, reviewed a variety of quotes, and have hopefully connected with a loan officer who offers good pricing and is responsive and trustworthy. Lenders all have their own procedures, but generally speaking, here's what happens next:

1. If you haven't already done so, you'll upload your financial documents to your online, secure portal.
2. You may be asked to pay in advance for your hard credit report. Some lenders require upfront payment; others include the fee in your closing costs.
3. Your application will be submitted for automated underwriting system (AUS) approval. Once approved, your file and documents will be sent to the processor.
4. Your processor will send your initial loan package for your signatures. This package includes a Loan Estimate, an Intent to Proceed, and dozens of other disclosures and authorizations. If you have any questions, reach out to your loan officer before you sign. Also, confirm that the numbers on your Loan Estimate match the numbers in their quote.
5. Your processor will review the conditions in your AUS approval and reach out for any additional documents that may be required, as well as payment for your appraisal. Do NOT pay for or approve the appraisal until after your inspection and repairs have been negotiated with the seller!
6. While waiting for your appraisal to be delivered, your file will be sent for initial underwriting. Assuming you are approved, your processor

will receive a list of conditions that must be met before you can close on the property.

7. Upon receipt of your appraisal and all other required documents, your file will be sent for final loan approval. Once final approval is received, you're cleared to close (CTC). Your file is then passed to the closing department.

8. At this point, the lender will most likely send you an early Closing Disclosure (CD) for your signature. An Early Closing Disclosure (CD) is a draft of the final mortgage loan statement that allows you to review loan terms, projected payments, and closing costs *before* the mandatory 3-day waiting period begins. This version of the CD is not yet balanced with the title company; expect many items to be missing regarding your title fees, escrows, pre-paids, and seller credits. Lenders say they send this version of the CD to catch errors. In reality, they send it to satisfy the 3-day waiting rule. That's okay. The balanced/final CD is often not distributed until a day or two before settlement/closing.

9. Loan documents will be delivered to the settlement or title company, who will arrange your signing.

Red Flags

Not every lender has your best interest at heart. As the mortgage market becomes increasingly competitive, many red flags appear early in the process. If a lender is pressuring you to make a quick decision, giving you vague information rather than a firm quote, or asking for payment information up front, slow things down. And be on the lookout for the scams and red flags discussed on the following pages.

YSP Rip Offs

You already know that lenders can get paid on the front-end, the back-end, or both; we also discussed how lender credits/Yield Spread Premiums (YSPs) can be a great way to reduce a borrower's out-of-pocket cost at closing. Countless borrowers use YSPs strategically to secure a home loan and purchase a home. From this point of view, YSPs aren't a problem. However, YSPs don't have to be disclosed to the borrower, and that's where the ethics become questionable (although perfectly legal).

Let's say you agree to a 30-year loan at 6.5 percent; you tell your loan officer to lock the rate. Since interest rates change daily, your loan officer might not lock in your interest rate right away. They can "float" your loan until there is a slight dip in rates, say, to 6.35 percent. Since you already agreed to pay 6.5 percent, they will lock you in at 6.5% and take an extra commission for selling you a 6.35% loan at a higher-than-market interest rate. Or maybe you told them to lock at 6.5% in the morning, but a few hours later, the rates dropped. You're sent a lock agreement at 6.5% and an updated Loan Estimate; you're not notified of the lower rate. Since YSPs aren't required to be disclosed to the borrower, you have no idea what happened. An upfront and ethical loan officer would have rebated you the YSP as a lender credit or offered you the 6.25 percent interest rate. Since the lender is not required to disclose this extra profit, you are none the wiser. Illegal? No. Icky? I think so.

What's a borrower to do? Ask your loan officer to re-price your loan before you lock. I always send my borrowers a screenshot of my rates so they can see what I see. I'm 100% transparent with my clients about rates, closing costs, profits, etc. It's not unreasonable for you to expect the same from your loan officer.

Collect Money Upfront to Keep You from Shopping

Some lenders may tell you that you can't receive a Loan Estimate without a hard credit pull, and they require immediate payment upfront for an appraisal when you haven't yet found a home. Collecting money from you makes it less likely that you'll walk away and use another lender.

Lenders *do* have the legal right to request payment for a hard credit report upfront, and with the alarmingly high cost of credit reports these days, they are more likely to do so. However, a hard credit pull is *not* required to receive a Loan Estimate, no matter what you're told. It can wait until you've found a house and selected a lender.

Any lender can do a "soft" credit pull, usually at no cost to you. A soft credit pull provides the lender with the same information as a hard pull, but it doesn't affect your credit score. By contrast, a hard pull reduces your credit by a few points, and the inquiry stays on your report for two years. A hard credit pull will certainly be required to process your loan application. But during the shopping phase, a soft pull at no cost is sufficient.

Note that a hard credit pull *is* required to run automated underwriting. If you have concerns about your qualifications because of credit issues or non-standard sources of income, it's far better to pay for a credit report to learn if you have preliminary underwriting approval BEFORE you spend money for inspections and earnest money.

YOU get to dictate when your credit is pulled and by whom. Control the process and don't agree to pay for a thing until you're comfortable doing so.

Intent to Proceed Violations

Lenders are required to receive your "Intent to Proceed" before they can begin to process your loan and collect money from you for anything more than a credit report. You need to explicitly state - via phone, email, text, or by signing an Intent to Proceed document – that you want to move forward with your loan application. Implying your intent is not enough. It needs to be an explicit statement, such as "I'd like to move forward with your 30-year fixed conventional loan."

Some lenders – particularly online lenders and banks – run on autopilot. They operate under the assumption that if you complete their loan application, you fully intend to use them as your lender, without exploring options or talking to other lenders. They run a hard credit pull. If you've given them a property address, they order the appraisal without your permission. Some have even scheduled their unauthorized appraisal before the home inspection was completed!

Don't be shy about telling the lenders you speak with that you're shopping around and that you do NOT want them to order an appraisal. Always keep your agent in the loop regarding your loan and the lender you choose. They can help intercept unauthorized appraisals.

> *What's a borrower to do? If this happens to you, send an email or letter explicitly stating that you did not give them consent to proceed and that you are cancelling your application. Tell them to stop all work immediately. If you've been charged for an appraisal or other services, demand a refund. Keep copies of all emails, call logs, and documents to prove you did not give consent.*

Quoting Rates Without a Loan Application

Interest rates are borrower specific and based on the lender's risk. Some lenders will quote rates without calculating or even asking about your income or credit. They talk about first time homebuyer programs without knowing if you make too much money to qualify for that program. Or they quote you a rate based on a 25% down payment and an 800-credit score, when you're planning to put 10% down and have a 680-credit score.

Not knowing your financial status allows a loan officer to promise low rates to capture your business; later, after your loan application is reviewed and your income is calculated, you learn that you don't qualify for the programs they originally mentioned. Since you've already paid for a hard credit report and have uploaded your docs, you stick with them even though you've been duped. That was their plan all along.

> *If a lender quotes you low rates without discussing or verifying your income and credit or quotes a rate without also providing a list of the associated points and closing costs, consider it a major red flag. Major.*

Advertising Super Low Rates

All businesses like to put their best foot forward in their advertisements, and the mortgage industry is no exception. There's nothing wrong with that.

When advertising interest rates, lenders must also display the APR associated with that rate in the same font size as the interest rate. *Nearly all lenders comply with this rule since the consequences of not doing so are severe.*

The problem with these ads – aside from the inaccurate and inconsistent APR calculations we discussed earlier – is that the advertiser decides the terms of the loan they wish to advertise. Since their goal is to advertise the lowest possible rate, they post rates for loans with huge down payments, well above average credit scores, and short payback periods. Most people will never qualify for this rate, but it makes their phone ring. Once you're in their web, you feel obligated to stick with them when they tell you that you don't qualify for the advertised rate. You feel bad that you don't make the cut; they act like your best friend who is going to work their magic to get you a loan. Illegal? No. Icky? Absolutely.

Underestimate Escrows and Pre-Paids

Any itemized loan quote you receive will include estimates of your upfront and monthly tax and insurance payments. An unethical loan officer can use ridiculously low figures for property taxes, insurance, and mortgage insurance to make their monthly payment appear to be lower than the next guy. Borrowers who focus only on the estimated monthly payment will be in for a big surprise when they get their actual payment amount.

It's very important that you are comfortable with your monthly PITI payments. But don't assume that the numbers quoted to you on a Financial Worksheet are accurate. They probably are not. And, when comparing mortgages, follow the procedure outlined above and ignore the number listed in the pre-paids and escrows section.

CHAPTER SEVEN

Preparing to Close

After repairs have been agreed upon and you have submitted a formal loan application to your lender, things can get very quiet. Some buyers become very anxious during this time and mistakenly believe that nothing is happening when, in fact, many things are happening behind the scenes. All the items below must be completed and approved before closing.

Title Work

Several people may have owned the property you are buying and even more may have owned the land. This historical record of ownership is called the "chain of title," which traces the property's history of ownership from the original owner to the current owner. When a contract is executed and placed with a title company, one of their first tasks is to perform a "title search" to confirm the title is clear and insurable. Title searches and policies are discussed in the next sections.

Title Search

The title search examines public records such as deeds, tax liens, and court judgments to verify the property's rightful, legal owner and to reveal any claims against the property that may affect its sale. It is a crucial step in the homebuying process that protects both the buyer and lender from hidden claims against the property.

If, for example, a previous owner had forged a signature (perhaps that of their former spouse), or there were unpaid taxes or other liens, there is a "cloud" on the title. The title search will reveal any clouds on the title that need to be cleared before the property can be sold. Title searches are required for any real estate transaction that requires title insurance; mortgage lenders require both a title search and a lender's title policy to underwrite the loan.

Title Commitment

After conducting their initial title search, the title company will issue a "title commitment," which informs the buyer and lender of any potential issues with the property's title. It itemizes the title defects, liens, and other issues and ensures the seller has the right to sell the property. It also lists any exceptions or exclusions the title insurance policy won't cover.

Pay particular attention to the "Clear to Close" section or Schedule C of the title commitment, which itemizes all title-related issues that must be cleared before a clear title can be conveyed and a title insurance policy issued. The title company may require information regarding the marital status of one of the parties, copies of records from probates or bankruptcies, clarification of homestead status, or a new or updated survey. You will also find descriptions of mortgages, mechanic's liens, tax liens, judgments, lawsuits, assessments, and other encumbrances affecting the title. The seller is primarily responsible for resolving these exceptions. After closing - when all the parties have signed, the deed is recorded, and all parties have been paid, the title commitment will be converted to a title policy.

Title Insurance Policy

Title issues can arise after closing, even with the most meticulous public records search. You might not learn about them for months, or even years, after your purchase. Some common examples of risks covered by your title policy include title defects caused by:

- Improperly executed documents
- Recording or indexing mistakes
- Forgeries and fraud
- Undisclosed or missing heirs
- Unpaid taxes, assessments, judgments or liens
- Unreleased mortgages
- Mentally incompetent grantors on the deed

Your lender requires title insurance to protect the mortgage amount, but it doesn't protect you or your equity in the property. For that, you need an owner's title policy for the home's value. In many areas, sellers pay for owner policies as part of their obligation to deliver a good title to the buyer. In other cases, borrowers must purchase it as an add-on to the lender policy.

Title insurance is critical! Don't buy a home without it!

Appraisal

An appraiser is a licensed, objective, third-party to the transaction. The appraiser's job is to give their professional opinion of the market value of a home. Lenders use the appraised value to determine if the value and property are sufficient collateral for a loan and to determine common loan ratios that factor into the loan approval process, such as loan-to-value, or LTV.

Appraisers are assigned randomly by an Appraisal Management Company (AMC), so neither the buyer, seller, nor lender can choose the specific appraiser for their property; the AMC selects from a pool of qualified appraisers based on location and availability.

Your lender will order your appraisal after your due diligence period has ended. In most (but not all) cases, an in-home visit is required; the appraiser will contact the agents involved in the transaction to arrange access to the property. About a week later, the appraisal report will be delivered to your lender with their opinion of its value. If the appraiser has concerns about the structural integrity of the property, they might recommend an engineer's evaluation of the property and/or repairs. For FHA loans, the FHA appraiser will make sure the property meets their required standards for safety, soundness, and security. These standards ensure the house is habitable, structurally sound, and free of health hazards. If not, the appraiser may recommend – and the lender will require – that those repairs be made before the closing of the transaction.

When you receive your appraisal, compare the square footage listed on the MLS and tax rolls to the measurement reported by the appraiser. Discrepancies in the reported property size are common and can arise from different measurement methods, inaccuracies in the source of listing information, or an appraiser's more thorough measurement process. Minor differences in square footage between the MLS and appraisal are often not a major concern, especially if the appraiser explains their methodology. If the discrepancy is significant, it can impact the final sales price and your financing. You may have the right to renegotiate the sales price or cancel the contract; talk to your agent about the appropriate next steps.

Appraisal Waivers

It's becoming more common for lenders to offer borrowers an appraisal waiver. An appraisal waiver allows qualified homebuyers to decline an appraisal. Rather than a traditional home value evaluation performed by a local appraiser, the lender will use computer-based valuation models and prior home value data to determine the property's value. A waiver can save you hundreds of dollars and may allow you to close more quickly.

Fannie Mae and Freddie Mac set the rules and regulations regarding who is eligible for appraisal waivers and which properties can qualify. To be considered, you must be a strong borrower with an excellent credit score and verifiable available assets. The dwelling must meet specific qualifications as well.

Be aware that your lender may require an appraisal at any time they reasonably believe it is necessary, even after the appraisal waiver is in place.

The rules for an appraisal waiver are detailed and continually modified. Speaking with a qualified mortgage lender is the best way to find out whether you qualify for an appraisal waiver.

Survey

A property survey is a sketch or map of a property showing its boundaries and other physical features. It also helps identify encroachments by neighboring properties, determine whether you can install a shed or swimming pool, and locate underground power, water, and sewer lines beneath your home.

Some states allow the seller to share their survey with the buyer if there has been no substantive change to the property. If this is the practice in your state, and the seller has a survey to share, it can save you hundreds of dollars.

To complete a survey, the surveyor will visit the property and sketch the land, its boundaries, easements, sidewalks, alleys, and other features that make up your property. This is known as the "fieldwork." You will be given several copies of the survey at closing. Keep your survey in case you decide to install a pool, sprinkler system, or other permanent structure on your property, and please pay it forward and share your survey with the purchaser of your home. The savings are substantial.

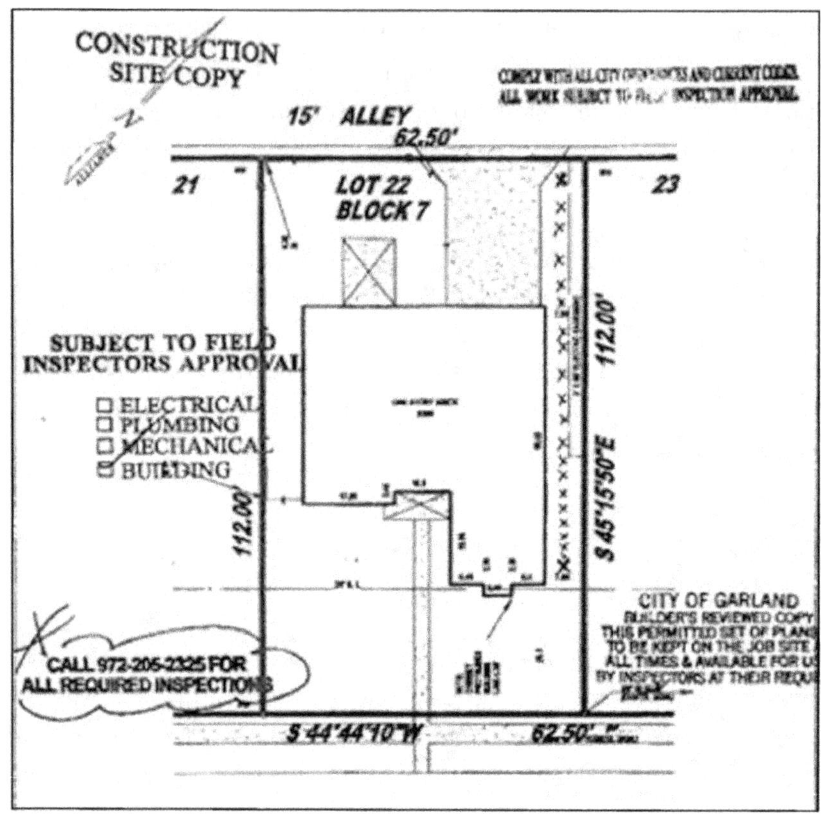

Homeowner's Association (HOA)

If you are buying in a neighborhood with an HOA, the association will be notified of the sale, a resale certificate will be created, and the account will be transferred to your name, pending closing. If the seller has any outstanding fees or fines, the title company will pay them out of the seller's proceeds.

Your contract can be written so that the HOA "covenants, conditions, and restrictions" (or CC&Rs) are sent for your review and approval before closing. If you have concerns about living in a neighborhood with an HOA, it's wise to review these documents during your due diligence period. This topic was discussed in detail in the contingencies section of this book. After closing, you'll receive an invoice directly from the HOA when the fees for the following year are due. HOA dues are not held in escrow.

Homeowner's Insurance

You are responsible for obtaining homeowner's insurance before closing; your loan won't be approved without it. Homeowner's insurance protects a homeowner against loss from fire, wind, hail, theft, freezing pipes, and other hazards that may impair the value of their home.

It is much easier to shop for homeowner's insurance than a mortgage because, unlike interest rates, premiums don't change daily. Hence, the price you are quoted is likely the price you will pay at closing. The amount you pay for a homeowner's insurance premium depends on several factors, including:

- the type of property you're buying,
- the cost of rebuilding it,
- the coverage amount,
- and the provider you choose.

In shopping for the lowest premium, you should be very careful to compare apples to apples. Compare two items: the *deductible* and the *coverage*.

The "deductible" is the amount of loss that the homeowner is responsible for. Only losses above that amount are insured. Higher deductibles carry lower premiums; lower deductibles carry higher premiums. The "coverage" dictates the maximum loss the policy will pay. There are four levels of coverage:

- actual cash value (lowest coverage)
- replacement cost
- extended replacement cost
- guaranteed replacement cost (highest coverage, but not always available).

Higher coverage carries higher premiums. Lenders typically require coverage equal to 100% of the replacement cost or the loan's unpaid principal balance, provided it equals at least 80% of the replacement cost value of the improvements.

Call several insurance agents for quotes or use an insurance broker to shop for you. When you have made your selection, have your insurance agent send a "binder" to the title company and lender. The title company is responsible for collecting money from you and paying for the policy at closing. If you establish an escrow account, your lender will also collect two to three months of premiums to fund your account. At the year's end, your mortgage company will pay your insurance bill.

If you buy a home in a flood zone, your lender will require flood insurance, which will increase your home's insurance costs. You should also be aware that most home insurance policies don't cover flood damage. To make sure your property is covered, you might need a separate flood policy.

Home Warranty

A home warranty is a contract between a home warranty company and a homeowner that provides discounted repair or replacement coverage for a variety of home items. You can choose your level of coverage to include basic items like the furnace, air conditioning, plumbing, and electrical systems, or add coverage for appliances, pools, refrigerators, and more.

If something in your house that was operable on closing day fails, you'll call the home warranty company; they will send over the right service provider for the job. The repair is made, or the component is replaced, and you pay only the cost of the service call, usually $60-100.

There are many different home warranty companies and many different levels of service. There are varied exclusions in their contracts, so review them carefully when you make your selection, and match the right coverage to the house you are buying. For example, if the water heater works but is a little dated, be sure you pick a provider who is more likely to replace it.

Keep your expectations realistic. If you're buying a fixer-upper, don't expect a warranty company to upgrade your entire home for you. But if you have an unexpected leak, broken appliance, or electrical problem, they provide a nice safety net and could save you a substantial amount of money on the required home repair.

I always negotiate a home warranty for my buyer/clients (except for new homes); your agent should too, unless the home you are buying is in pristine condition with mostly new components. Reviews are mixed for even the most popular home warranty providers, but in my view, it's better to have one than not.

Pre-Closing Walk-Through

A pre-closing walk-through is a final inspection of the home before closing, and I recommend two, when possible. The first should be done 24-48 hours before closing to verify that all agreed-upon repairs have been completed (get repair receipts in advance) and to ensure there has been no damage to the property since you were last there. *You do not want to wait until an hour before closing to express dissatisfaction with the home's condition, as the seller needs time to make corrections.*

The second walk-through should be conducted immediately before closing to ensure everything is in order before you sign your documents. This is something I generally do for my buyers, since they are busy at the bank and often come right from work. The second walk is just to make sure the house is still standing and hasn't been vandalized. It is exceedingly rare for something like this to happen, but better safe than sorry in my view.

If you uncover a major issue with the house during your final walk-through, delay closing. Once you sign the documents, any issues become your responsibility.

"Major" means something significant, such as an air conditioner that doesn't work, a house that was vandalized, a hailstorm that damaged the roof, and similar conditions. The house must be returned to you in the same condition you last saw it in, and the repairs must be completed in accordance with the terms of the contract. Otherwise, don't close until everything that was promised to you is delivered.

If you have minor issues, your agent can negotiate a repair credit for you to make the repair after closing, or the title company can hold back some of the seller's proceeds in escrow until the issue is resolved. It is during times like these that you need a good agent to represent your interests.

Temporary Lease Backs

It can be risky for a seller to move out of their home before closing and funding. If the buyer fails to close after the seller vacates the property, the seller faces a huge problem. For this reason, many sellers won't (or can't) move until after the sale has been finalized. This can create problems for buyers who have just purchased a home while someone else is still living there. What if they refuse to move?

> *Unless you're buying a vacant home, you absolutely must have the sellers sign a temporary lease agreement, which means they are your tenants until they move out.*

Under a proper lease, the seller can be evicted if they refuse to vacate. Without one, removing them from the property can be a lengthy legal battle. Ensure the lease specifies that the house must be left in clean, move-in condition. The word "clean" is subjective, of course. I generally suggest that buyers plan to hire a cleaning service and carpet cleaners before moving day. You might be lucky and have a seller who leaves you a spotless house, *but don't count on it.* Last-minute issues related to their move might prevent even the cleanest sellers, with the best intentions, from leaving the home as clean as they would like. Sometimes they are lazy, but often, they are just busy. Plan for the worst-case scenario.

CHAPTER EIGHT

Closing Day

The "closing" (aka settlement) is when the paperwork is signed, and all funds are disbursed. A title company or settlement company facilitates the process. In some states, attorneys are present, and the parties sign simultaneously; in others, attorneys aren't necessary, and the buyers and sellers never meet.

As a neutral third party to the transaction, the settlement company has many responsibilities, including:

- Receiving and holding the buyer's earnest money and option fee in a trust account
- Managing the paperwork between the buyer's agent and the seller's agent, the lender, insurance companies, and home warranty providers.
- Coordinating the funding of the loan
- Paying off the seller's loan
- Assisting in the preparation of the Closing Disclosure
- Disbursing the seller's checks and the agent's commissions
- Prorating annual property taxes and other obligations
- Ensuring the buyer can receive clear title to the property

Once your loan is fully approved and you are clear to close, your lender will send loan papers and closing instructions to the title/settlement company, and the parties will work closely to balance your final Closing Disclosure (CD) and finalize all the documents that are to be signed at settlement. Let's take a closer look at the most important documents.

Closing Documents

Buyers sign a huge stack of papers at the closing table; sellers only sign a few. The ones that you should pay close attention to are described in detail below.

You usually don't have time to reach every word of every document at the closing table. If you'd like to review the documents in advance of your signing, ask your lender and closer to email you a secure copy of your closing docs the day before you sign.

The Closing Disclosure

By law, you must receive a Closing Disclosure at least three business days before closing, although some lenders send a preliminary (unbalanced) disclosure to the buyer as early as 10 days before closing. Doing so ensures compliance with the three-day TRID rule and allows you to close on time. Providing the buyer with this important information well ahead of closing also gives them time to understand their loan costs in a relaxed environment, rather than at the closing table. Frantic, last-minute trips to the bank to get a cashier's check or wire money an hour before closing are eliminated, and parties have sufficient time to troubleshoot mistakes.

The Closing Disclosure is five pages long and, like the Loan Estimate, very easy to understand.

The *first* page is like the first page of the Loan Estimate and includes information identifying the borrower and loan, loan terms, monthly payments, and the total closing costs and cash required to close.

The *second* page lists closing costs and indicates who pays each cost: the borrower, the seller, or another party.

The *third* page includes the cash needed to close and a summary of the borrower's and seller's transactions.

Pages *four* and *five* contain additional loan disclosures and contact information for the creditor, brokers, and settlement agent. The additional disclosures address whether the loan is assumable, negative amortization information, late payment fees, escrow requirements, and more. The fifth page also calculates the total payments, finance charges, financed amount, and interest percentage over the loan term. Finally, the fifth page also contains a signature block for consumers to confirm receipt of the disclosure.

Compare your Loan Estimate with the closing statement to see how close your lender's estimate was to the actual figures. If there are any big surprises, discuss them with your agent and lender immediately. Also, be certain that you received a credit for any deposits you put down for earnest money, any option fees, prepaid appraisals, and so forth. Your agent should be well-versed in this document and can assist you. You will need to bring a cashier's check or wire funds in the appropriate amount to closing, along with a photo ID. Be sure to keep your funds readily accessible in a local account.

> *Don't wait until closing day to figure out how you'll send your funds to the title company. Plan ahead!*

A sample and annotated Closing Disclosure can be found on the supplemental documents page of my website.

Promissory Note

A promissory note is your promise to repay your mortgage. It outlines the mortgage terms and conditions and is typically signed at closing. Without a legally binding promissory note, the lender has no recourse if you fail to pay your mortgage. Promissory notes are used in mortgage transactions in every state, regardless of whether the state primarily uses mortgages or deeds of trust (discussed in the next section).

Although the structure of a note can vary from state to state, they typically include:

- Names, addresses, and signatures of the borrower and lender
- Principal loan amount
- Interest rate
- Lump sum or installment payment amount
- Payment due date and schedule
- Late fees or other penalties

You are expected to comply with the repayment terms set out in this document. If you fail to do so, the lender has the right to recover its money through the foreclosure process described in detail in your Deed of Trust or Mortgage, depending on your state.

*The promissory note is one of the few **very important** documents you sign at closing. Review it carefully before signing to ensure it is 100% accurate. If it's not perfect, do not sign! Your settlement officer or closer will work with your lender to make any necessary changes.*

Deeds of Trust/Mortgage

If you don't pay, you don't get to stay. Depending on where you live, at closing you'll sign either a Deed of Trust or a Mortgage that describes in detail what happens when you don't pay your mortgage.

The difference between a mortgage state and a Deed of Trust state concerns how home loans are secured and how foreclosures are handled. In a mortgage state, the lender and borrower use a mortgage to secure the loan. This document pledges the property as collateral for the loan. The property is also pledged as collateral in a Deed of Trust state, but these states require an additional party (a trustee).

Foreclosure in a Deed of Trust state is typically handled through a non-judicial process, which is faster and less costly. By contrast, in a mortgage state, the lender files a lawsuit, and the court oversees the foreclosure process to ensure it is done legally. This can take several months or longer.

Some states use forms that are "promulgated", meaning the document is an official, standardized form that is legally binding, and the use of the document is mandatory to ensure legality. Other states use state-approved forms created in conjunction with local Realtor associations to ensure fairness to all parties to the contract. If you're buying a home in a state that uses standardized forms, consider yourself lucky since you won't need to hire an attorney to review your contracts (although you always have the option to hire one).

IRS Documents

At closing, the primary IRS-related documents you will sign to verify tax information for your lender include IRS Form W-9 and Form 4506-T.

IRS Form W-9 confirms your social security number/taxpayer ID for reporting mortgage interest and property taxes. Be sure the information on this document is accurate so that you can deduct the interest and taxes you pay on your income tax return.

Form 4506 authorizes the lender to request tax returns directly from the IRS. It acts as an anti-fraud measure, allowing lenders to verify your income, tax filing status, and accuracy of submitted W-2s or tax returns before approving a home loan. Lenders typically require you to sign this at the beginning of the application and again at closing for a final review.

Warranty Deed

A warranty deed (signed only by the seller) transfers property ownership from the seller to the buyer and guarantees that the seller has a clear title, the legal right to sell it, and that it's free from undisclosed liens, claims, or encumbrances. It provides the highest level of buyer protection and allows buyers to hold sellers accountable for future title issues.

The purchase of a title insurance policy transfers accountability from the seller to the title company. If there is a claim against the title of your property and a title policy is in place, it will be the responsibility and expense of the title company to defend and resolve the claim.

Initial Escrow Statement

An initial escrow account statement is the first mandatory disclosure from a loan servicer detailing the estimated taxes, insurance premiums, and other anticipated charges to be paid from a borrower's escrow account during the first 12 months of the loan. It includes the monthly escrow payment, the total amount to be disbursed, and any required initial cushion. Legally, the lender has 45 days to provide your initial escrow statement, but you will most often receive and sign it at closing. At the end of each year, you will receive an Escrow Analysis Statement which details the money you paid into your escrow account, the money paid out of your account to cover your property taxes and insurance, and a statement of escrow projections for the following year. If there is a surplus in your account, meaning you paid more than necessary to cover your expenses, your escrow payment will be lowered for the following year. If there is a shortage, meaning you didn't pay enough or the cost of taxes or insurance has increased, your escrow payment for the following year will rise.

Affidavits and Declarations

Affidavits and declarations signed at real estate closings are sworn written statements that verify the accuracy of specific things. Sellers commonly sign affidavits confirming that no new liens, unpaid repairs, or undisclosed tenants exist, while buyers sign declarations stating that they intend to occupy the property as their primary residence and are not purchasing the home as investment property. Buyers also confirm that they have not committed loan fraud, accept the property in its current condition, and that any name variations found in public records and credit reports are accurate.

Cash to Close

Your Closing Disclosure will indicate the amount you need to pay in certified funds or by wire transfer to the title company. Be sure to confirm which payment methods your closer accepts.

A cashier's check is a paper check issued by your bank and made payable to the title company. The teller will verify your identity and ensure you have sufficient available funds to cover the check; there may be a small fee involved. You will deliver the check to the title company at closing, or a few days prior, if required.

Due to an increase in fraudulent cashier's checks, some lenders no longer accept them as a method of payment.

If your bank is not local, you can initiate a wire transfer by phone, in person, or online. A wire transfer is not immediate, so plan accordingly. Wire transfers are convenient but can present drawbacks. Money can get lost, or the numbers can be transposed. If you miss that day's wire deadline, your funds won't be sent until the following day, which may delay the funding of your transaction. The manager who must approve the wire might be out and unavailable that day.

Title companies will NOT accept ACH transfers. Funds must be WIRED.

Play it safe and wire the funds a little early. If the thought of wiring such a large sum gives you anxiety, transfer a small amount like $20 first. Confirm that the transfer was successful before sending the balance.

If you are wiring funds, you must CALL the title company to confirm their wiring instructions. Do NOT rely on the information you receive in an email, regardless of the source!

Scammers have intercepted hundreds of thousands of wire transfers, resulting in millions of dollars in lost closing cost funds! You are going to be warned about this over and over and over again. Please be careful and take it seriously.

Funding

Once the buyers and the seller have all signed the papers, the title company and lender review the signed documents to ensure all the required signatures and initials have been received. Then, the monies are wired from your lender to the title company. The title company uses this money to pay off the seller's mortgage (if any), the insurance companies, the real estate agents, and any other party to the transaction entitled to receive payment. This process is called "funding". Once funding is finalized and approved, the house is officially yours!

You are not allowed to receive your keys until funding is complete, so if you plan to move the same day you sign, plan accordingly. It's always better to sign in the morning to allow time for the funding process to happen. If a temporary lease agreement is in place, you may take possession in accordance with its terms. Your agent will arrange for the delivery of the keys to your new home.

Recording

The recording process is the final step in the closing process; it involves filing notarized documents with the county court's office to give public notice of the lien against your property. It establishes the lien's priority and protects the lender's interest against other creditors. The closing company, attorney, or title company that handles your transaction will complete the recording process. Failure to record can lead to issues with title, ownership disputes, and challenges for future sales.

Once your mortgage is paid off, either through the sale of the property, a refinance, or by the homeowner, a release of lien is recorded which removes the lien from your property.

Recording fees are calculated per page and are included in your closing costs.

CHAPTER NINE

After the Close

The stress involved with buying a home can strain even the toughest individuals, and your accomplishment is worth celebrating – in a very big way! Drink the champagne and enjoy a nice meal. Then, follow the guidelines below to protect your investment and ensure your future happiness.

Immediate Next Steps

First things first. Use the checklist below to ensure a smooth transition into your new home.

- Secure the Property - Change all exterior door locks immediately; you don't know who has a copy of the old keys. Also, reset the garage door code and the alarm codes.
- Transfer Utilities - If you haven't already, set up your electricity, gas, water, and internet services.
- Deep Clean and Paint - It is much easier to clean, paint, or refinish the floors when the house is empty, before your furniture arrives.

- Purchase Appliances - Measure the laundry room and space where the refrigerator will go. Keep in mind the refrigerator will require 1/8"-1/4" for airflow around the unit to prevent overheating. Also, be mindful of the refrigerator's depth. A counter-depth unit has a sleeker, more modern look and improves kitchen traffic flow. A standard depth can store more food, but it protrudes 6 or more inches past the counters, making the kitchen feel smaller and interfering with foot traffic.
- Locate shut-off valves: Know how to shut off your water, gas, and electricity so you can act quickly in case of emergency.
- Store Closing Documents - Find a safe place to store the closing package you received at settlement. If possible, keep a secure digital copy as well.
- Purchase a folder or binder to hold house-related manuals, receipts, paint colors, etc.
- Change Your Address - Notify USPS, your banks, credit card companies, employers, and insurer of your new address, and change your address on your driver's license.

Paying Your Mortgage

Your first payment is usually due a full month after closing. If you close in April, for example, your first payment is probably due June 1st. Look for a welcome letter from your loan servicer with specific instructions but call to confirm the information before sending them your first payment. Nearly all services offer autopay and online options for paying and tracking your monthly mortgage payments. Establishing an online account will help ensure your payments are made on time and will prevent you from incurring expensive and unnecessary late fees.

Do not be surprised if you receive a letter from the lender stating that your loan has been sold; this is a common practice. If this happens, your current lender will send a goodbye letter and tell you where to send your payments. You should also receive a hello letter from the new lender, now your loan servicer. It's always a good idea to confirm the sale with your current lender before sending money to a new lender. Call. Confirm. Be sure.

The loan servicer will track your payment history, apply your monthly loan payment to your loan balance and escrow, and pay your annual property taxes and hazard insurance from your escrow account when they become due. While the tax and insurance bills should be sent directly to the loan servicer, they may also be sent to you. If so, just forward them to the servicer for payment, or call them to confirm they received their own copy.

As discussed earlier, your payment may increase or decrease in the future if a higher or lower escrow balance is needed to meet rising or falling real estate tax or insurance costs. The loan servicer will provide a year-end interest statement and an account analysis so you can monitor your account. You will also need this information when you file your taxes to ensure you take the appropriate deductions for the interest and real estate taxes you have paid.

Homestead Exemptions

Most states offer exemptions that could help you reduce your property tax bill and receive protection from creditors.

State, federal, and territorial homestead exemption statutes vary widely. Some states, such as Florida, Iowa, Kansas, Oklahoma, South Dakota, and Texas, have provisions that allow 100% of your home equity to be protected. Other states, such as New Jersey and Pennsylvania, do not offer any homestead protection. The degree of protection in New York varies by county.

Homestead exemptions work by reducing your home value in the eyes of the tax assessor. So, if you qualify for a $50,000 exemption and your home is worth $300,000, you will be taxed as if your home is worth only $250,000. In most cases, people with permanent disabilities, veterans, seniors, and spouses of veterans can qualify for additional exemptions that reduce their tax bill even further.

Depending on your location, you may be able to file for your homestead exemption online with your county's appraisal district; the deadline is usually in March or April. You'll need to provide documentation showing you qualify, such as your driver's license (with your new address), military papers, tax returns, etc.

If you forgot to file your exemption paperwork, you could still apply up to two years retroactively, but you'll have paid higher taxes in the meantime. It's far better to address this task as soon as you've updated your address on your driver's license.

Prepaying Your Mortgage

Prepaying part of your mortgage allows you to pay *a lot* less in interest over the life of your loan. For every extra dollar you apply toward your loan principal, you save about two dollars in interest. For example, on a $200,000 loan with a five percent interest rate, paying just an extra $50/month will save you almost $21,000 over the life of the loan, and the loan term will be reduced by almost three years. That means your 30-year loan becomes a 27-year loan. An even greater result can be achieved by making one extra mortgage payment each year, reducing your loan term by about 7 years!

In addition to saving on interest, paying your mortgage early allows you to build home equity faster. That means you'll be able to pocket more money when you sell and, if you're paying private mortgage insurance (PMI), you can eliminate it sooner. Even though a mortgage is generally considered "good debt," you may want to pay it off for peace of mind if your financial situation changes, or as part of your retirement planning preparation.

If you decide to prepay your mortgage, don't sign up for the "bi-weekly prepayment program" that your lender will offer you. These programs require a setup fee of about $300-400, plus a $5-8 monthly service charge. You can prepay at no charge in almost all cases. Just add the extra amount to your normal monthly payment or pay it separately to make it easier to audit later.

*Be certain that you indicate to your lender, in whatever format they require, that your extra payment is to be applied toward the **principal only**, not interest!*

Here Come the Scams!

When you buy a house, the deed is recorded with the county and becomes part of the public record. Businesses compile mailing lists of people who recently bought a home and try to sell them a wide range of products and services. The junk mail is endless! On the plus side, you do receive lots of valuable coupons to furniture stores, home improvement centers, and many other retail establishments, so keep your eyes open for those if you're a coupon cutter. But be on the lookout for the following scams, described next.

Homestead Scams

Filing your homestead exemption is free in most states. Scammers will send you very official-looking documents with filing instructions and charge you $25-$150 to record the documents for you. Don't fall for this! Just go online to your county's appraisal district and look for filing instructions. It's a simple process that takes only a few minutes and costs you nothing.

Mortgage Scams

Be on the lookout for companies that want you to send them your mortgage payment, claiming that they will make your payment for you. The problem is *they don't!*

If you ever receive a letter stating that your loan was sold or transferred to another bank and that you should start sending your payments to a different address, call the old bank to verify this information before making your next payment.

Mortgage Protection Insurance (MPI)

Mortgage protection insurance, sometimes called mortgage life insurance or mortgage payment protection insurance, is designed specifically to pay off a mortgage if the homeowner dies during the term of their loan. Some policies will also pay if the homeowner is permanently disabled.

Don't confuse Mortgage Protection Insurance with Private Mortgage Insurance or PMI. PMI is a policy that covers the *lender* in the event of default. MPI covers the *homeowner*.

One of the biggest problems with MPI is that the coverage amount decreases over time as you pay down your mortgage, while your mortgage premiums remain the same. In addition, these policies are solely for the purpose of paying off your mortgage. Your family can't use the funds for living expenses or college tuition.

You are generally better off buying a normal term life policy and/or disability insurance. Mortgage insurance policies are overpriced and sometimes underwritten by less-than-reputable insurance companies. What good is insurance if the company is bankrupt when you need it?

Predatory Refinancing

Predatory refinancing occurs when a lender uses abusive, deceptive, or high-pressure tactics to convince homeowners to refinance their mortgages into loans with extremely high fees, unaffordable terms, or high interest rates. Here are some common tactics:

- Loan Flipping: Repeatedly refinancing a loan within a short period of time, paying new points, high fees, or increasing the principal balance.
- Equity Stripping: Encouraging cash-out refinances that drain a homeowner's equity, particularly when the lender knows the borrower cannot afford the new and higher payments.
- Hidden or Excessive Fees: Tacking on high closing costs, broker fees, and pre-payment penalties to a refinanced loan.
- Bait and Switch: Advertising favorable terms but switching to a much more expensive loan product at closing.

If you're considering a refinance, be on the lookout for lenders with high-pressure sales tactics, "no cost" refinancing, no credit checks, and those offering a refinancing option with no tangible benefit to you, like a lower interest rate.

> *Thanks to TRID, lenders are no longer legally allowed to refinance a home when there is no net benefit to the homeowner — but it still happens. That's why they call it "fraud".*

Foreclosure "Rescue" Scams

A foreclosure rescue scheme is a scam targeting homeowners in default on their mortgages; it offers the false promise of saving their homes from foreclosure. Scammers often take equity, charge upfront fees for no service, or trick owners into signing over deeds. These scams typically result in the homeowner losing their property and more money. Common types of foreclosure rescue schemes include:

- The "Phantom Help" Scam - Scammers charge exorbitant fees for simple, free services like filling out paperwork or making phone calls, often promising false loan modifications.
- Foreclosure Rescue/Bailout Scam - Con artists trick homeowners into signing over the property deed, promising they can stay as renters and buy it back later. They then take the equity and often evict the residents.
- The Bait and Switch - Homeowners are deceived into signing documents they believe will bring their mortgage current, but which transfer ownership to the scammer.
- Fake Counselor/Lawyer - Scammers pose as lawyers or housing counselors, requiring you to make payments directly to them rather than your legitimate lender.

If you are having trouble making your mortgage payment, contact your lender as soon as possible to discuss available options. Avoid any business that:

- Provides a money back guarantee that says they can stop the foreclosure
- Advises you not to contact your lender
- Tries to collect a fee from you in advance
- Only accepts a cashier's check or a wire transfer
- Advises you to make your mortgage payment directly to them
- Tries to get you to transfer your title

Most lenders have no interest in foreclosing on your home! Don't panic if you fall behind; act quickly and deal only with your loan servicer, not a third party.

Contracts for Deed

A contract for deed is commonly used with seller financed transactions. Under a contract for deed, the property title remains in the seller's name until the buyer has made a certain number of payments, and sometimes until the buyer has paid off the house in full. Although the seller is supposed to transfer title to the buyer after the buyer has paid off the mortgage, this doesn't always happen. In essence, buyers are paying for a house they will often never truly own. Contracts for deed are a great deal for the seller but are a nightmare for the buyer. Steer clear.

Seller-financed transactions REQUIRE the use of an attorney. Always. No exceptions.

Rent to Own

Rent to own transactions work like this: If a buyer can't qualify for a traditional mortgage, a seller might agree to rent the house to the buyer for a period while the buyer gets their finances in order. At the end of the lease term, they buy the house through traditional financing, at a predetermined price (top dollar). The buyer typically pays a large option fee upfront, and a portion of the monthly rent is applied toward the home's sales price.

In theory, it sounds great. More often than not, however, the buyer doesn't qualify for their loan and loses their option fee and any potential equity in the house. Or the terms of the purchase are so outrageously expensive that it doesn't make sense to move forward with the purchase.

Renting and buying should be treated as two separate transactions, not rolled into a single transaction.

If you can't qualify for a traditional mortgage, rent until you can. If you insist on a rent to own transaction, hire a lawyer, not a Realtor, to handle the paperwork. Most of us are not qualified to protect you in these transactions, and we're not dumb enough to try.

Note that a rent to own differs from a lease option, although the concept is the same. A lease option usually doesn't require a large upfront payment, only first and last month's rent. You agree to buy a property at a preset price after leasing it for a period, but if the property value goes down, you don't have to purchase the property. Depending on the state, lease options do not allow a portion of your rent to be applied toward your down payment. Instead, you pay rental amounts that are substantially higher than market and lose all the money you paid should you choose not to buy the home. I'm not a fan of this idea either.

Rather than getting involved in a financial transaction that's almost certainly doomed to fail, I suggest you talk to a lender about what it will take to qualify for a mortgage. Don't call a subprime mortgage with high rates and fees; use a traditional FHA or conventional mortgage lender and let them advise you. There's no shame in renting until the time is right for you to buy.

Rental Scams

Scammers have been hijacking rental ads by changing the contact information and reposting the modified ad on another site. Or they create rental listings that don't exist. The goal is to get you to pay a security deposit or the first month's rent before you realize it's a scam.

Beware of anyone who tells you to wire money or if they want a security deposit or first month's rent before you've met or signed a lease. Try to confirm the identity of the person who is showing you the home.

Reverse Mortgages

Reverse mortgages allow homeowners aged 62 or older to borrow against the equity in their home, with no repayment required until they move out or die. But scammers have devised about 5 or 6 ways to steal the equity in the homes of unsuspecting seniors. With promises of free loans to finance expensive vacations and other luxuries, some lenders are aggressively pitching to homeowners who cannot afford the fees, let alone the property taxes and maintenance on their homes.

Reverse mortgages can be a valuable tool for seniors to stay in their homes and access their equity, but choosing the wrong lender is a recipe for disaster. If you're in the market for a reverse mortgage, be on the lookout for high pressure sales tactics, tricky advertising, understating the risk of losing the home, and being asked to leave your spouse off your loan.

CHAPTER TEN

What Can Go Wrong

Buying a home is a high-stakes marathon where things can go wrong at any stage—from initial budgeting to the final signing. Your file/transaction will be handled by 10-15 people between contract signing and closing, and even though all parties share the goal of closing the deal, things can go wrong.

The most common pitfalls often involve financial miscalculations, structural surprises, or last-minute legal hurdles. Keep reading for some examples.

Financial & Lending Fails

- Taking on new debt (like buying furniture or a car on credit) or even switching jobs after being approved can cause a lender to rescind their offer right before closing.
- The title company does not receive documents in time for closing.
- Buyer loses their job, so their loan is denied.
- The lender cannot clear the borrower's loan conditions in time.
- If the appraisal comes in lower than your sales price, the lender will not cover the difference. You may have to pay the gap in

cash, negotiate a lower price with the seller, or restructure your loan.

- Simple typos in names or misspellings of addresses on legal documents can halt the process while new documents are drafted and notarized.
- Scammers may impersonate title companies to send fake wiring instructions. If you wire your down payment to them, that money is often gone forever.

Inspection & Property Disasters

- Hail, wind, fire, vandals, etc., damage the property, and it needs to be reinspected.
- The survey shows an encroachment or other problem.
- During the final walk-through, new damage or theft is discovered, or the seller has removed items from the home that were supposed to remain, such as appliances.

Seller Related Issues

- The title search finds a lien against the property, and the seller does not have the cash to clear it.
- The seller changes their mind or refuses to move.
- The seller is buying a new home, and there is a problem with that transaction.
- The seller dies.

Some things are just beyond anyone's control, so there is no point in worrying about the improbable things that can go wrong. Resolving these issues requires extensive communication, some compromise, and levelheaded real estate professionals on both sides. Do your part, and more than likely everything will work out in the end.

CHAPTER ELEVEN

Final Thoughts

There you have it...what you need to know about buying a home. Yes, it is complicated and sometimes stressful, but it is worth the time you invest in reading this book to educate and protect yourself.

Start by hiring a great agent to represent you and never sign anything until you have a thorough understanding of your risks, responsibilities, and rights. Don't be a lazy buyer!

Most of all, know that before long, you will be moving into your new home, and the stress of the homebuying process will be long forgotten. You will be putting down roots and becoming part of a new community. Many, many firsts will take place in your new home, and countless memories will be created.

My hope is that I have helped you avoid the horrible, gut-wrenching, stress-inducing buying process, and that you will have many years of happiness in your new home. Feel free to contact me at Main@HelpUBuyAmerica.com if you have questions about the process, your mortgage, or need a referral to an Exclusive Buyer's Agent in your area.

About the Author

Alysse Musgrave is the owner and CEO of HelpUBuy America, an Exclusive Buyer's Agency and mortgage company that has been working to protect people from predatory lending and other shady real estate business practices for over 31 years.

As a graduate of Texas A&M University, Alysse has taken the Aggie Code of Honor: "An Aggie does not lie, cheat or steal or tolerate those who do" and has applied it to her work in real estate. As the moral and ethical foundation of HelpUBuy America, adherence to this code has led to an outstanding record of customer satisfaction.

When she's not busy protecting homebuyers from unethical business practices or training new agents to uphold the principles of honesty and integrity, Alysse is an avid reader, writer, sports fan, and beach bum. Instantly recognizable for her iconic monkey mascot, Alysse has authored 4 books and served as a regular contributor to Zillow Group, where she is a highly respected expert on homebuying, the real estate industry, and related topics.

www.ingramcontent.com/pod-product-compliance
Lightning Source LLC
Chambersburg PA
CBHW051801050726
47598CB00006B/2380